08-BVR-705

i pi_{d i}

Jacopo Fasolo

Another
Venice

arsenale et editrice

Jacopo Fasolo
ANOTHER VENICE

drowings and text
Jacopo Fasolo

layout
Stefano Grandi

printing
EBS Editoriale Bortolazzi-Stei
Verona

first edition
May 2000

Arsenale Editrice srl
via Querini 100
30172 Venezia Mestre
Italy

Arsenale Editrice © 2000

ISBN 88-7743-216-0

Photo credits

Eugenio Rossaro, Venice: pp. 19, 22,
24, 26, 28, 30, 32, 40, 47, 51, 54, 56,
61, 64, 80, 84, 86, 92, 96, 108, 114,
134, 136, 139, 146, 150, 152, 154,
156, 166, 176, 178

Mark E. Smith, Venice: pp. 16, 34, 42,
44, 66, 70, 76, 78, 82, 88, 94, 98, 100,
102, 104, 110, 118, 120, 126, 130,
143, 148, 160, 164, 168, 170, 172

Contents

Introduction 7

General map 10

Locations 12

San Marco 15

San Polo 39

Santa Croce 75

Dorsoduro 90

Cannaregio 125

Castello 159

Bibliography 191

Introduction

"It almost seems difficult for me to admire this Venice: you have to start at the beginning to learn. Its marble is ashen, a pallid grey, as luminous as the edge of a coal that has just stopped smouldering. How inexplicable are the red of the walls and the green of the shutters; so restrained and yet impossible to ignore; it is the past, but in the fullness of flight; it is so pale, just as people turn pale as their emotions increase."

This is how Rainer Maria Rilke described Venice to his sister Clara in a letter sent from the Zattere on November 20th 1907. And it is not very difficult for us to comprehend his sense of admiring astonishment when faced with the kaleidoscopic complex that, almost inconceivably, forms and informs the city, based as it is on an element which is constantly in motion – water. This water breathes in unison with the ocean, permeates every nook and cranny of the city, constituting its roads and walkways and infusing the buildings with an ever-changing light, reflecting their image and constantly forging new forms. Each step is punctuated by exceptional motifs and a wealth of sensations that the ever-mutating situations of the light and water surfaces multiply and extend to the very limits of the surreal.

More than in other contexts, in fact, the visitor who doesn't want to limit him or herself to a superficial view of the city has to find a harmonious relationship with the city and come to terms with the spirit that living in Venice has always implied.

First of all there is the relationship with water, which informed the founders' defensive view of the city and which gradually went from being a conditioning element to a fundamental fixed premise for all subsequent developments and eventually constituted its beauty and characteristic diversity. Certainly, if you think of the building and organisational difficulties imposed by this element, you could not but agree with Diego Valeri, a much-loved Venetian poet, who affirmed that "our holy fathers, more than a thousand years ago [...] must have had not only an uncommonly iron will but also a touch of generous insanity".

Water was originally the only link between and within islands, which had not yet been interlinked and were simply uninhabitable muddy areas. The more the islands were colonised and built up, the more important the role and function of water became. So much so in fact that not even in the 13th century, when *land* became central in the construction of the streets, alleyways, foundations and bridges that linked series of large urban areas, did Venice abandon the centrality of water in terms of transport – in fact these large urban areas were still separated by large canals.

And the city's houses themselves give onto the water. The main entrances and façades face the lagoon or canals, while their "back yard", used for the delivery of day-to-day goods and containing gardens, were eventually "colonised" by a series of *corti, campi* and *campielli*.

The structure of the city, obviously conditioned by the surrounding water to such an extent that its very limits were determined by the surrounding lagoon, was characterised by innumerable superimpositions and layers which contain and encapsulate notions and elements taken from the various cultures the Serenissima came into contact with.

Considering the peculiar and multi-layered nature of this context, predefined and precise urban schemes could not be applied. And yet the beauty, truth and measure that are the lowest common denominators of the city's countless views, incredibly scenic spaces and veritable *coups de théâtre* of light and space in the *campi* and canals immediately make one think of an artfully construed orchestration of varied and multifarious architectural solutions and ornamental inventions.

The human dimension and the strong, direct relationship between the city's constructs and its inhabitants have always been respected in terms of the typically Venetian nature of the city's problems and the solutions found for these problems, fostering an awareness of having to suit the construct to the needs of the city – and all of this was perfectly in keeping with the relationship that the city's citizens had with the construct itself and a more general sense that the common good was the primary condition guaranteeing the survival of all.

Venice, more than any other city, is the end result of single particles which have been cemented together by a commonly-felt sense of danger and the city's own idiosyncratic nature. Venice has been considered a house that has to be shared by all, where no-one passively accepted choices made by the elected representatives of the city, where each individual felt as if they were participating in decisions that would effect the entire community, with a faith in a surprisingly swift and farsighted judicial system.

And Venice is still being inhabited with the same spirit: it is a large "shared house" where the *campi* are the rooms and the *calli* the corridors, where people bump into each other quite often and where relationships are established that are sometimes simply the end result of accidental meetings that take place as people move from one area to another in the city. As in any home, people are not afraid of getting lost as the house's size, despite the sometimes tortuous nature of some of the "corridors", is contained and allows its inhabitants to meet whenever they want.

Even the city's place-names mirror the directness that characterises living and working in Venice, reflect the events, customs and problems that characterise the different areas, and form a sort of account of the birth and growth of the city, bearing historical and conscious witness to the city itself. As such the place-names also underline the fact that events develop according to timeless principles and that the various interventions have been borne of the city's needs and the events it has had to deal with.

Thus we cannot but see Venice's architecture, whether it be humble or monumental, as forming a single unit that pulsates with the ideas of profound necessity and fully-fledged culture – each and every architectural manifestation therefore demands and deserves the visitor's close attention.

And this is a sign of the attention paid to "another" Venice, a Venice which is not exclusively monumental. In terms of the "readability" of its details and the smaller size of its buildings, this "other" Venice is perhaps much more accessible to us, much more intimate as well as fascinating and surprising in its more variegated solutions.

To see the buildings of this "other" Venice, you will have to climb into a boat and silently glide along the city's remoter canals, those without foundations. Only in this way will the buildings offer up their history and their *raisons d'être*. Even the smallest of canals hide buildings, *palazzi* and houses which blend into one another to create larger, more vaguely outlined agglomerations with their own correspondence of elements, motifs and colours.

Modern society, with its impelling need to contain both time and costs, with its habits and necessities, has rendered the older rhythms "extraneous", thus making the current city seem "anachronistic". But, in the words of Le Corbusier, *"Venise est aujourd'hui encore un admoniteur: circulations classées, royauté du piéton, échelle humaine, grandes conditions de nature imposées par l'élément: l'eau"*. There is still hope that it might be possible to find a new equilibrium based on acceptable links with the external world, allowing this extraordinary testimony to the ingeniousness of man to continue to live and allow man to live according to its message of civilisation.

General Map

Boat Stop ▲
Gondola ferry ■
Sestieri and other locations ● S. Marco ● S. Polo ● S. Croce ● Dorsoduro ● Cannaregio ● Castello

Locations

Location	Chapter	Page
Abbey of San Gregorio	38	118
Abbey and Church of the Misericordia	45	143
Arsenale	60	180
Calle del Paradiso	55	168
Calle Magno	59	178
Campiello Barbaro	35	108
Campiello Querini Stampalia	56	170
Campo dei Mori	44	139
Campo del Ghetto Novo – The Ghetto	43	136
Campo della Bragora	57	172
Campo di Rialto	18	64
Campo San Barnaba	29	94
Campo San Boldo	13	49
Campo San Geremia	41	130
Campo Santa Margherita	28	92
Campo Santa Maria Mater Domini	22	78
Campo Santi Giovanni e Paolo	52	160
Campo San Zan Degolà	24	82
Carampane	15	54
Casa Agnusdio	21	76
Casino Venier	2	19
Church of the Gesuiti	47	148
Church of the Tolentini	26	86
Church of San Giovanni Elemosinario	17	62
Church of San Giovanni Grisostomo	51	156
Church of San Nicolò dei Mendicoli	31	98

Church of San Pantalon	27	90
Church of San Pietro in Castello	61	186
Church of San Raffaele	32	100
Church of San Sebastiano	33	102
Church of San Simeon Grando	25	84
Church of Santa Croce degli Armeni	8	32
Church of Santa Maria dei Miracoli	49	152
Church of Sant'Aponal	16	59
Church of San Teodoro, Scuola di Sant'Apollonia	9	34
Convent of San Salvador	4	24
Convent of the Church of Santo Stefano	6	28
Corte Bottera al ponte del Conzafelzi	53	164
Corte Morosini	50	154
Fondaco del Megio	23	80
Fontego dei Tedeschi	1	16
The Frari	11	42
The Herb and Fish Market	19	68
Madonna della Salute	39	120
Ospedaletto	54	166
Palazzo Ariani	30	96
Palazzo Da Mosto (once known as Baglioni-Muti)	14	52
Palazzo Giustinian Faccanon	3	22
Palazzo Malipiero, Campiello della Feltrina	7	30
Ponte Molin de la Racheta	46	146
Ponte di San Giobbe (also known as dei Tre Archi)	40	126
Ponte di Cannaregio (also known as delle Guglie)	42	134
Ponte Donà and Palazzo Donà	48	150
Rio Terà dei Catecumeni	37	114
San Trovaso	34	104
Scoletta dei Tiraoro e dei Battiloro	20	74
Scuola dei Calegheri	10	40
Scuola di San Giorgio degli Schiavoni	58	176
Scuola di San Giovanni Evangelista	12	45
Scuola di San Girolamo	5	26
Le Zitelle, Giudecca	36	110

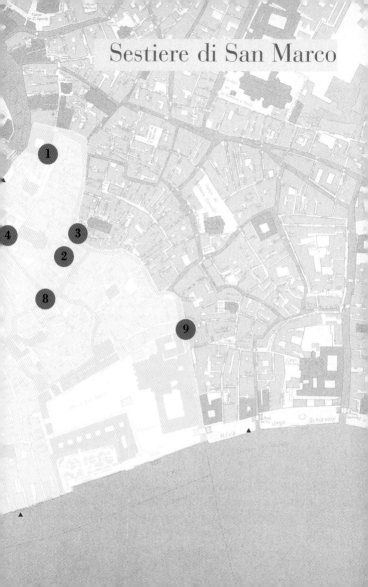

Sestiere di San Marco

1. Fontego dei Tedeschi

The *fonteghi* ("foundations") were buildings owned by the city of Venice but given over to foreign traders. They were originally intended to be used as goods warehouses, hospices, customs and commercial areas, and the Republic established regulations according to which they could be used. The *fonteghi* also had an ambassadorial function, and their location, size and architectural aspect in some way related to the importance of the foreign country. In the 16th century, the Fontego dei Tedeschi was, because of the amount of trade with Germany, the largest of the *fonteghi* and contained more than 200 rooms. It was located on the Grand Canal alongside Rialto Bridge and decked out with important works of art and external decorations. These characteristics were further enhanced by the reconstruction undertaken by Giorgio Spavento and Antonio di Pietro Abbondi, known as Lo Scarpagnino, which was completed in 1508. The façade was given two small lateral towers, and was decorated, like the side façade giving onto the Rialto Bridge, with a series of frescoes by Titian and Giorgione. Only a few fragments of these frescoes are still extant, and can be seen in the Accademia Gallery and Ca' D'Oro. The rooms are grouped around a large central court, surrounded by loggias on different storeys (the different floors were used as warehouses, offices and living quarters). There were also two large common-rooms: the so-called "Sala d'Inverno" (or "Winter Room"), called a *stua* (Venetian for "stove") because of its large gilded brass stove, and the so-called "Sala d'Estate" (or "Summer Room"), also called "The Treasure of Pictures" because of its paintings by famous 16th century Venetian painters. There was another room set aside for visiting German citizens, the so-called *grisolotti*, who were forced to stay in the room for reasons of public security.

Public and social activities were also undertaken in the *fondaco*, underlining just how open and accepting the Serenissima was to foreign habits, beliefs and customs. Three days before the beginning of Carnival, the Fon-

daco opened its doors to the city, and the indiscriminate in- and out-flux of masked merry-makers was so vast that it virtually contradicted the principle of "confinement" and "control" that had given rise to the idea of *fonteghi* in the first place.

Along with the Fondaco, Germans in Venice also congregated in the church of San Bartolomeo, where they had their own chapel, the altar of which proudly displayed Durer's altar-piece *Madonna with Rosary*, now in Prague. German-Venetian relations were always substantially good, both in terms of temporary visitors to Venice and those who had settled in the city for commercial reasons and contributed to forming that popular social and economic milieu that was so important for Venice's economic development. The activities of the Fondaco came to an end with the fall of the Serenissima.

The building was eventually handed over to the Internal Revenue Department, and then finally to the postal services. As the central post office of the city, the Fondaco still evokes that sense of business and noisy international hubbub that echoes its original function.

2. Casino Venier

The *casino* or *ridotto* belonging to Elena Priuli, the wife of the Venetian procurator Venier, was one of the many private "houses of pleasure" that were so common in 18th century Venice. It occupies the first floor of the *palazzo* on the corner just over Ponte dei Bareteri, with a balcony hanging over the Merceria del Capitello. The original decorations, fire places and wrought-iron balustrades are all still extant. The term *casino* was originally used for any "house" that provided refreshment, rest or just a room where you could change between important appointments. However, the *casino* also provided "special" services for both men and women who were interested in slightly more adventurous refreshments. There were also less exclusive *casini*, which were restricted to members belonging to the same social or commercial category. For example, there were *casini* for secretaries, craftsmen and the general public. Despite the fact that the Council of Ten often called for their enforced closure for reasons of decency, the number of *casini* continued to grow, especially after the Ridotto (a public gambling house near St Mark's) was shut. When the Republic fell in 1797 there were 136 *casini* in the city. Elena Priuli's Casino Venier was one of the more exclusive *casini*. From the completely windowed veranda, Elena Priuli would secretly observe the carnival revellers below. With her mask at the ready, she would wait until she spotted the "right" person, then she would go down into the street and lead the "victim" to her alcove. Unwanted visitors, who could be observed through a special hole under a tile on the first floor, would not be allowed any further than the ground floor entrance area. There was originally a secret exit, which has since been closed.

In 1987 UNESCO funded the building's restoration, and it is currently home to the central offices of the French-Italian Cultural Association, Alliance Française.

3. Palazzo Giustinian Faccanon

You will get the best view of the façade of the building from Campo della Fava. You can move in closer, although you will lose a full view of the façade, via Riva Tonda, which you can reach from the Marzaria di San Salvador, where Calle Delle Acque begins. The only other way to see the façade is by getting into a boat and moving in as close as possible from Rio di San Zulian.

This is an ogival *palazzo* from the second half of the 15th century, perhaps built after Ca' Foscari in the bend of the Grand Canal, the façade structure of which it actually repeats. Each floor is separated from the others by string-courses bearing diamond and cord-like decorations, and the corners are decorated with corded columns. The building has remained virtually unchanged throughout the centuries. The most important change was the addition of the attic floor (which takes away from the majesty of the façade with its crowning row of little 18th century statues along the balustrade), which the then-owner, Cavalier Faccanon, decided to add in the early 19th century. In 1872 the *palazzo* was temporarily given over to the central offices of the postal service. It was then used for a few years as the main offices of the Civil Service Workers Insurance Office, who, in the winter months, often organised musical performances, balls and even meetings and exhibitions in the *portego* on the first floor.

From 1898 to 1977 the building was the headquarters for the *Gazzettino*, Venice's local newspaper, and housed the newspaper's entire production team, including the printing works.

4. The Convent of San Salvador

The area between the church of San Salvador and the San Salvador canal, delimited by the houses along Calle del Lovo and Calle Delle Balote, is occupied by a monastery or convent annexed to the church. The first official reference to the buildings constituting this complex dates to the second half of the 11th century. The convent was enlarged in the 15th century, with numerous buildings aligned along the canal and articulated around two courts or cloisters. The mixed style of the buildings is due to piecemeal work and enlargements undertaken over the centuries. Towards the mid-14th century a radical restoration led to the buildings outlined in Jacopo de' Barbari's map, dated 1500. Between 1507 and 1534, the entire complex was transformed and rebuilt, thus bringing about the loss of its Gothic-Byzantine character, which was replaced by the current classically Renaissance forms. The project and direction of this renovation were Spavento's, even though he was replaced by Tullio Lombardo and, in 1530, by Jacopo Sansovino. Lombardo and Sansovino are considered responsible for completing the interior of the church and the convent's cloisters, which were finished in 1564. The church and convent were retained by the brothers of the St Augustine order, who were attacked by the priests of the nearby parish of San Bartolomeo, who accused them of licentiousness. The state of affairs improved only when the brothers were (forcefully) replaced by others from the congregation of San Salvatore in Bologna. In 1810, the parish of San Salvador subsumed that of San Bartolomeo, and the convent was transformed into a barracks. It has been maintained that Campo San Salvador once had "a deep well with a water trough and a tying-post nearby, to which, when horse-riding was still common in the city, travellers would tie their horses, as, following a decree dated February 24th 1287, horse-riding was prohibited along the Merceria, especially in consideration of the large numbers of people."

5. Scuola di San Girolamo

The Scuola di San Girolamo is one of the few small *scuole* to have maintained, at least in part, their original artistic heritage. In fact, because of its wealth and large confraternity, the *scuola* was upgraded in 1689 and put on a par with the six large *scuole* of the city. It was founded in 1471, when two confraternities, San Girolamo and Santa Maria della Giustizia, were fused into one. The original two confraternities were both dedicated to helping prison inmates, and especially those on death row, whom they would accompany to the gallows in lugubrious processions. This *scuola* was therefore called Scuola di Santa Maria della Giustizia (or Justice) e di San Girolamo, and was also known as the Scuola di Santa Maria della Consolazione (i.e. "consolation"), and popularly known as the Scuola Dei *Picai* ("the hanged") or *Della Buona Morte* (i.e., "of merciful death").

The current Scuola was built at the end of the 16th century by Alessandro Vittoria. The Istrian stone façade has two Classical orders, with Baroque-like decorative and *chiaroscuro* elements. The Scuola was suppressed in 1806 and in part stripped of its contents. It was then reopened in 1810 as the headquarters for the Veneto Society for Medicine, and in 1812 it became the Veneto University for the Sciences, Arts and Fine Arts. The external area just in front of the façade is currently used by the nearby restaurant for its outdoor tables. This has contributed to giving the *campo* its feel of an open-air living-room, especially during the evening hours, where people flock from all directions along the diagonal paths which offer very interesting views of the perspectives afforded by the buildings. Unfortunately, the views are currently somewhat limited by reconstruction work undertaken on the Fenice, which was destroyed by fire on January 29, 1996.

6. Convent of the Church of Santo Stefano

The Santo Stefano convent occupies the area that includes the church, the *campanile* and Campo Sant'Angelo. It was founded by the Augustine Brothers, who arrived in Venice in about 1000, and built between 1294 and 1325. Originally, the convent's entrance was through the doorway on the left as you observe the church façade. Later, an entrance was also opened up from the *campo* over a private bridge that was linked to the bridge leading to Calle dei Frati in 1455. The convent's original structure comprised only two cloisters. However, as early as the 15th century it began to be enlarged and was given much more embellished decorations. The larger of the two cloisters, destroyed by fire in 1529, was reconstructed according to the Renaissance style by Scarpagnino in the 1650s, and was completely frescoed by Pordenone with scenes from the New and Old Testaments. The frescoes, unfortunately, are no longer extant. The second cloister's 14th century aspect is still admirably intact, however. It can be reached from the apse area of the church, and is near the *campanile* which, even before it was completed in the 16th century, began to lean. It was because of this that the *campanile* was not given a concluding spire until 1544, even though the pinnacle arch was never completed. The *campanile* began to lean even more dramatically in the 17th and 18th centuries, and to make sure it didn't suffer the same fate as the *campanile* in Campo Sant'Angelo, annexed to the no longer extant church of San Michele Arcangelo (the *campanile* collapsed twice in the 14th century, killing a handful of monks), the Santo Stefano *campanile* was reinforced and its foundations enlarged. Corte Cavazzera along Rio Malatin, just behind the church of San Maurizio, affords an incredible view of the entire *campanile* and its reinforcements.

The convent, which was suppressed by the French in 1810, is currently the head offices for the Finance Ministry and the State Accounts Department.

7. Palazzo Malipiero, Campiello della Feltrina

The building on the Santa Maria Zobenigo canal, which can be seen on the right as you walk over Ponte Duodo into Campiello Della Feltrina, is Palazzo Malipiero. The *palazzo* is an example of the High Gothic style which developed in Venice in the second half of the 15th century and that has much in common with Venetian civilian Gothic. It is characterised by the "compositional completeness" of the exterior and a squared quadriforate window, with squat late-14th century columns. Venetian authorities sometimes allowed subject cities from the mainland, such as Brescia, Bergamo or Chioggia, to have their own buildings in Venice so as to be able to host important guests from their own city. With the passing of time, the communities in question employed people to look after their buildings, who would then rent out the rooms to anyone, regardless of their origins. In June 1502, a law was passed to "remove such persons from these houses" and to prohibit new custodians from cooking on the premises or accepting money. Palazzo Malipiero was one such building, and belonged to the city of Feltre. Despite the above-mentioned legislation, the house was given over to a private "manager" who used it as a hotel, as can be deduced from a legal battle between hotel proprietors published in the *Giornale Veneto* on April 24, 1786. The judge's final sentence confirmed that the only real "hostel of the city of Feltre" was Palazzo Malipiero, located between the two bridges at Santa Maria Zobenigo.

8. Church of Santa Croce degli Armeni

Of all the foreign communities in Venice, the Armenians were the last to have their own centre in the city. Because of the constant persecution suffered by Armenians at the hands of the Turks, numbers of refugees increased and the community became one of the largest and wealthiest in Venice. According to the Republic's economic and political system, all foreign communities were given hospitality and residency rights, with very stringent operative limits within which, however, they were also guaranteed absolute freedom, but were not allowed to assimilate with the rest of the population. Armenians began to arrive in Venice in the second half of the 13th century, and documents attest to the fact that they had their own parish house in San Zulian in the San Marco area, where they also had a hospice and their own oratory.

In 1675, thanks to funds bequeathed by the community, the San Marco Procurator gave permission for renovation work on the building. The new building also contained a church. It is very likely that the project was put together by Giuseppe Sardi. The new church was allowed to keep the name of Santa Croce di Cristo, that is the same as that of the old church, which was a simple chapel built in 1496. The church is not that easy to spot from the outside, except for the lantern set atop the cupola and the small *campanile* flanking the church. The church has no façade because the other houses belonging to the community are built so close to the building. The entrance can be found in the Sottoportico della Calle degli Armeni. Inside, there is only the one square-plan room, surmounted by a cupola, which was given a narthex form designed to echo older Byzantine architectural forms. Architecturally, the elements are very elegant and restrained, with characteristics that can best be described as classical rather than Baroque. The church is still maintained by the San Lazzaro brothers, and can be visited only on Sunday mornings during the service.

9. Church of San Teodoro and Scuola di Sant'Appollonia

After Piazzetta dei Leoncini, turning right at the end of Calle Della Canonica, you will come to a bridge of the same name. Once you've gone up the large steps that lead from the Fondamenta to the bridge proper, you will find a doorway leading to the church of San Teodoro (also known as the church of Sant'Uffizio) and the San Pietro chapel, with a passage that runs the length of the apse area of St Mark's Basilica. The little church, which is partially subsumed within the Doge's Palace, was built in 1486 in Renaissance style according to a project by Spavento. Construction was so quick that in 1491 Tommaso di Giorgio was already busy frescoing the façade, which has since unfortunately been reduced to mere brickwork. The space available for the building, which was originally planned as a chapel, was further reduced in the 16th century when Sansovino's buttresses were added to reinforce the Basilica. The current, hardly harmonic space of the façade (which has been given no apparent order) is made all the more curious by the addition to the buttresses of fragments of architectural marble belonging to different styles and periods which were brought to light during restoration work undertaken on the basilica. The hotchpotch effect is a perfect example of the Venetian expression *"andar per le fodere"*, that is reaching hidden areas by following secret paths, thus heightening the visitor's sense of discovery and expectation.

Even the Doges sometimes felt the need for secret, alternative routes, although admittedly this was probably for security or state reasons. In fact on Easter Sunday of 864, Doge Pietro Tradonico was assassinated during the traditional walk to the church of San Zaccaria along Riva degli Schiavoni. The same fate befell Doge Vitale Michiel II on Easter Sunday 1171. For security reasons, it was decided that Doges would henceforth wind their way to the church of San Zaccaria by following a route that went through Campo Santi Filippo e Giacomo, (the bridges of the Canonica and San Provolo were thus built). The Doge left from the doorway that also leads to the church of San Teodoro. Just beyond Ponte della Canonica, along Fondamenta di Santa Appollonia, in the building facing the canal and the large Renaissance wall of the Doges' Palace, there is a white stone doorway with a carved architrave and cord-motif internal corners. This is all that remains of the church of Santi Filippo e Giacomo, whose beautiful Gothic façade, with is mixed linear crowning piece containing niches and spires, could last be admired towards the end of the 18th century. Towards the end of the Fondamenta, however, you can see what remains of the monastery dedicated to Santa Scolastica – a magnificent cloister. The original name, however, is now hardly ever used: because of its proximity to Ponte della Canonica, where there was once the Scuola dei Linaroli (or linen-workers), whose patron saint was Santa Appollonia, Appollonia's name was eventually extended to the monastery as well, thus replacing the original Santa Scolastica. The 13th century Santa Appollonia cloister is the oldest in the city, and is the only surviving example of Romanesque architecture in Venice. The cloister is exactly as it originally was, save for the fact that it was slightly raised to guard against flooding in the 17th century. The plan is rectangular with terracotta pavements both in the portico and the courtyard, where the Byzantine-style well can be seen. The cloister contains robust single columns and light paired columns holding up double terracotta arches of different heights, on a continuous stone-covered terracotta base, with a central passage on either side with two Istrian stone steps leading to the central area of the cloister.

The building, restored in 1964, currently houses the Marciana Basilica Museum.

Sestiere di San Polo

10. Scuola dei Calegheri

One of the aims of the *scuole* or confraternities was to set up a corporation for the organisation and defence of a group's production activities and to provide apprenticeships and even assistance to members of the confraternity and their families in case of need. These *scuole*, mainly "minor" in terms of number of members and the social status of the category, eventually grew in number and began to represent all crafts, and were sometimes even sub-divided into smaller specialisations (so that, for example, *marangoni*, or carpenters, were further subdivided into those working on houses, furniture, frames, panelling and so on). The Scuola dei Calegheri (i.e., cobblers), had its main offices in Santo Stefano and another, very beautiful set of offices which can still be seen at San Tomà. The San Tomà building, bought in 1446, was finalised by 1478, which is when the façade was finished, with its marble lunettes (by Lombardo) representing St Mark and St Anthony, patron saints of the *calegheri*. The *calegheri* placed their altar, which up to then had been in the Carità church (now the Accademia), in the church of San Tomà in 1446. Each cobbler in Venice, whether he was a *calegher* (maker of new shoes) or a *zavater* (maker of slippers) had to be a member of the confraternity and pay membership fees. As there were no associates or rich merchants, the only income on which the *scuola* could count came from these fees, donations from other members and payments for church candles. Considering the *scuola*'s limited finances, the decorations for the *scuola* were all undertaken by the members themselves. Proof of this can be seen in the painting that the Scuola commissioned in 1556 and which is now in the Museo Correr: the painter, obviously, is anonymous.

From 1446 the *calegheri* were given the privilege of presenting the Doge's wife with a pair of shoes on the occasion of the feast of the Ascension (known as "The Sensa" in Venetian).

11. The Frari

The term *frari* seems to be a contraction of *"frati minori"*, or "minor friars", that is those belonging to the Franciscan order, who arrived in Venice in about 1222 (according to Bonaventura da Bagnoregio, St Francis himself came to Venice that same year). The Frari, however, refers to the church and convent complex, which is one of the largest in the city along with Santi Giovanni e Paolo. When the order had been in Venice for a while and had grown in number, they were given leave to occupy a pre-existing Benedictine abbey in the same area, and in 1236 Doge Jacopo Tiepolo gave them the so-called "lago Badoer" (i.e. the "Badoer lake"), a swampy area near Rio San Stin (St Stephen the Confessor). A first church was built between 1250 and 1280, with the apse facing Rio dei Frari. In 1340, work began on the current church, which was originally dedicated to Santa Maria Gloriosa. The building was completed in about 1445 (the *campanile* was finished in 1396). The first church was demolished in 1415, which was replaced by a second church placed transversally where the first had stood. According to a curious anecdote, the Franciscans who had the Frari bridge built in 1428 demanded that the area be allowed to offer immunity to delinquents simply because "the Church of the Frari was there, and that was where the large chapel was, which has since been turned". The bridge was completely rebuilt in the 19th century, and conserved only the original Gothic frame and the Franciscan coat-of-arms.

The convent was built along the western wall of the church and, in the first half of the 14th century, a refectory and chapter-house were built around the first cloister. The library, the school and a hospital for the brothers were subsequently added. The order's general synod was held in Venice in 1346, and the convent put up 1,500 brothers. In the 15th century, the complex was called "Ca' Granda" ("the large house") because of its size, and in 1500 Jacopo de' Barbari depicted the complex

in its current form. A second cloister, dedicated to St Anthony, was added to the first, dedicated to the Holy Trinity. The new cloister backed on-to the convent of San Nicolò and its church (now demolished) and clois-ter (since annexed to the Frari complex). The two cloisters were fin-ished in the 16th century according to Renaissance canons, and have tra-ditionally been attributed to Palladio and Sansovino, with 18th century additions to the Holy Trinity cloister by Pittoni.

The importance of the Frari to the city and the fascination it exerted on the different classes in the city is attested to by the fact that the com-plex is surrounded by no fewer than five *scuole*: to the right as you look at the façade were the Scuola dei Fiorentini and the Scuola di Sant'An-tonio; to the left, in the vicinity of the small Renaissance *palazzo* not look-ing over the Rio, the Scuola della Passione (which was moved to the site from San Zulian in 1572); and finally another two *scuole* in the single-storey building that delimits the *campo* running parallel to the Rio – Scuola dei Milanesi and Scuola di San Francesco. Each of these *scuole* had an altar in the Frari church, which also contained works of art com-missioned by the *scuole* themselves (the altar of the Scuola dei Fioren-tini, for example, had Donatello's *St John the Baptist*, which is now in the right apse chapel).

Between 1806 and 1810, Napoleonic law outlawed religious institutions and confiscated their property. The buildings once used for religious pur-poses were then forced to house socially-useful institutions such as schools, hospitals and museums. In 1815, the convent, along with the San Nicolò complex and the Scuola di Sant'Antonio, were used as the State Archives. After restoration work, the site was used to house centuries' worth of doc-uments from the city's Councils, the judicial system (for both public and religious offices) and the accounts of the fallen Republic. Still now, after further renovations, the centre is being used as an archive, available for consultation and research. It has been estimated that in the 280 rooms of the centre there are more than 700 million documents collected in more than 15 million volumes.

12. Scuola di San Giovanni Evangelista

One of the most interesting aspects of civil, social and religious life in Venice, whose very structure seems to promote a more communal type of social interaction, is that of the confraternities or *scuole*. Some *scuole* were organised according to devotional principles, some for artists and craftsmen, and others according to ethnic and geographically-defined principles. The former were mainly devised to help others, while some, and especially the latter, were organisations for specific categories of workers. In the 13th century, the *scuole* were divided, according to their size and the qualification or prestige attached to their members by the bourgeoisie, into major and minor *scuole*. There were a great deal of *scuole*: in 1501, Sanudo counted 210 *scuole* with their insignia who were present in St Mark's Square for the funeral of Cardinal Zen. Of these, only five were considered major: the Scuole of San Marco, San Giovanni Evangelista, San Rocco, Misericordia and Carità. The Scuola di San Teodoro was added to this exclusive list in 1552, and the Scuola dei Carmini in the 17th century.

The Scuola di San Giovanni Evangelista, dedicated to St John the Evangelist, was founded in 1261 as the confraternity of "flagellants", and was based in the church of Sant'Aponal. It moved to its current site in 1307, that is a church dedicated to St John the Evangelist and founded in 970 by the Badoer family. The church originally had only one altar and one chapel. In 1340 it rented a few rooms in the hospice that the Badoers had founded just in front of the church, and which was radically renovated by the church itself in 1340-45. In 1369 Andrea Vendramin, the *scuola*'s Grand Guardian, was given a relic of the Cross, which greatly added to the prestige of the *scuola* and its confraternity. The activities of the *scuola* and its subsequent greater income meant that in 1414 the school not only needed to but was also able to buy and restore an old hospice. Over the years the hospice was further restored and enlarged

by the confraternity, which began a period of uninterrupted prosperity. The Scuola is an admirable example of the harmonious mix of styles which developed in Venice over the years, from High Gothic to the Renaissance, and which were simply superimposed on each other without in any way clashing. In 1454 the Gothic side façade was added, in 1481 the Renaissance doorway by Lombardo, in 1498 the double-ramp Renaissance staircase and Cordussi's two double-arch windows with a central oculus giving onto the canal, in 1568 the altar in the Sala della Croce. Some time after 1572 Massari designed the oval windows and had the main hall raised to eleven metres. The magnificence of the architectural improvements was equalled by an imposing collection of art works, the most important examples of which included the *Miracle of the Cross* cycle by Gentile Bellini and Carpaccio (now in the Accademia). The architectural complex of the Scuola di San Giovanni Evangelista constitutes a unique urban context. It is almost like a series of Chinese boxes, made all the more interesting by the character of the individual areas and volumes, the quality of the works and the mixture of styles. To those who arrive via Calle Zane, Campiello San Giovanni will appear in its entirety in its perspectival axis – its small size will allow you to take in the entire set of elegant lesenes on three sides, the exquisitely carved marble flag-holder, the doorway and windows of the septum which flows naturally into the next space. And this space, it could be argued, constitutes the pronaos of the *scuola*'s little *campo*, which is much larger and more severe and which leads to the church to the left and the *scuola* to the right, closed off by the transversal septum and Palazzetto Badoer with Sottoportego della Lacca. Up to the 19th century, the doorway to the septum had a gate, and the courtyard that is now open to the public was once closed off and private.

This Scuola, like the others, was suppressed in 1805 and, partly deprived of its art works, was transformed into a warehouse. Renovated by its new owner, Gaspare Biondetti, it was restored to its religious status in 1857 and given over to the Building Workers' Society for Mutual Assistance. It is currently used for social events and art exhibitions.

13. Campo San Boldo

Campo San Boldo is closed off on two sides by Rio Boldo, and on the other two by Palazzo Grimaldi (17th century) and other houses. Palazzo Grimaldi is flanked by what remains of the *campanile* attached to the old church of Sant'Ubaldo, popularly known in Venetian as "San Boldo".

The remains of the *campanile* is all that is left of the old religious complex. The church was built in about the year 1000 and originally dedicated to St Agatha. During the complete restoration undertaken in the early 14th century, the *campanile* was built, and decorated with delicate little blind arches and spires. The church, which was completely reconstructed between 1735 and 1739, was closed in 1805 and demolished in 1826. The pollarded *campanile* was turned into a residence.

The area is also characterised by the unexpected way in which it opens out where the canals meet, affording a rare "opening" in the otherwise tight weave of the city. The *campo* is well and truly off the beaten track now, mainly because, after a few of the *rii* in the area were filled in, it now no longer provides a direct route between Campo San Polo and San Giacomo Dell'Orio. Its recently-found tranquillity certainly adds to its allure and fascination.

Popular tradition has it that women would once flock to the church to pray to St Agatha, to whom the church was also dedicated until the 16th century and who was martyred when her breasts were removed.

14. Palazzo Da Mosto (once known as Baglioni-Muti)

On Canale di San Cassiano, between Ponte della Malvasia (once known as Ponte Zanandrea della Croce) and Ponte de le Tete, you can see the imposing façade of Palazzo Muti, which was subsequently called Palazzo Acquisti, then Palazzo Verzi, Palazzo Baglioni and finally, in 1919, Palazzo Da Mosto. Ponte de le Tete was given its somewhat unique name ("tete" means "breasts" in Venetian) when the Serenissima, apparently in an attempt to dissuade its male citizens from the rather popular vice of homosexuality, gave the prostitutes of the area permission to show their bare legs and breasts on the bridge in order to attract clients. The enormous *palazzo* was built in the early 17th century. It was considered by its contemporaries to be one of the most interesting *palazzi* not on the Grand Canal, both in terms of its construction and decorations. The façade on Calle de Ca' Muti or Ca' Baglioni is different from the one on the *rio* only in that it is developed along a broken line. Apart from this, both façades have three doorways, two central Serliane, with a sculpted bust over the central doorway, Ionic capitals on the first floor and Corinthian capitals on the second. In 1737 the building was badly damaged when the house next door burned down, and Baglioni decided to take advantage of the restoration to add the windows along the mezzanine and just under the line of the roof. The two side doors originally gave onto lateral corridors, which were apparently once the two little alleys that separated the *palazzo* from the neighbouring houses and then subsumed into the Palazzo itself.

It is impossible to get a complete view of the building except from some of the private buildings above which Palazzo Da Mosto seems to tower. But even when seen from the street below (and perhaps even more so from the entrance alley, which gives you a very good angled view of the central Serliana) the imposing façade has the overwhelming presence of a large wall of illuminated rock, especially at sunset.

15. Carampane

Carampane is the name of a courtyard that is found at the far end of Calle dei Boteri, opposite Riva dell'Olio, the *fondamenta* on the Grand Canal in front of Ca' D'Oro. This courtyard, ensconced within a very tight weave of houses, links a *sottoportico* and series of very small alleys with Rio Terà de le Carampane.

The name, however, really refers to a much larger area, the nucleus of which lies between Callesella Carampane, Calle Drio le Carampane, Rio Terà de le Carampane and part of Rio de le Becarie. The houses in this area were once owned by the patrician Rampani family, and Ca' Rampani is the name of the house on the Rio Terà with a Renaissance doorway and a triforate window and partly blind quadriforate window on the façade. The above-mentioned street names all obviously derive from the family name.

But the name itself has also taken on the meaning of "prostitute", and not of the high-class "courtesan" type, defined as "honest and honourable" prostitutes, but rather of the much more "downmarket" variety which the Venetians also called *mamole* and *bagatine* (from "*bagatin*", the name of one of the smallest coins). To understand why this family name became associated with prostitutes we have to go back to 1358, when the Republic asked the so-called "heads" of each Sestiere to find appropriate premises for all Venetian prostitutes in the Rialto district (chosen because its enormous crowds made it one of the ideal spots in the city where prostitutes could ply their trade). A block of houses in the parish of San Matteo was eventually chosen because it had only one entrance. It was given the name of Castelletto, or "small fortress", and was considered an ideal place for a brothel. A few "madams" were chosen to keep track of all profits, which were distributed equally amongst the women at the end of the month. During the day, the prostitutes were allowed to work outside Castelletto in the Rialto area and in Campo delle Becarie, but they had to return before the third round of bells rang from St Mark's (i.e. between 9 and 10 p.m.); those who did not were severely whipped. Castelletto was closed on all religious feast days, and there were six "custodians" whose job was to make sure that the prostitutes obeyed the numerous rules and regulations. Despite these regulations, the prostitutes would often "wander" into other areas of the city, and one of their favourites was the series of houses owned by the Rampani family. The name of the area thus became synonymous with prostitution and prostitutes. Prostitution, however, even for an "enlightened" city like Venice where it was considered a necessity that had to be kept in check but not prohibited, was a serious problem. In fact, prostitutes constituted an enormous social "class" unto themselves, and at the beginning of the 16th century there were 11,650 prostitutes out of a population of about 160,000 inhabitants. They constituted some 30 % of all sexually active women in the city, and one of the most worrying aspects was that some of these women were nothing more than mere girls. This led to a plethora of sometimes contradictory measures aiming to deal with various problems as they arose. One of the most perverse aspects of this situation was that, for example, while the Serenissima attempted to limit the scope of prostitution for reasons of morality and public security, at the same time it also issued guidelines on how and where prostitutes should bare their "legs, breasts and other bodily parts" in a bid to foster a "healthy" heterosexuality amongst male citizens who the Serenissima was afraid had

developed an "unhealthy" proclivity for homosexual practices and sodomy. There were also different rules for different classes of prostitutes (the higher class of prostitute, or "courtesan", was often merely reprimanded, and sometimes even publicly "protected" by lawmakers), and laws designed to curtail prostitution were often quashed lest the public revolts of the (male) citizens they provoked should get out of hand.

Be that as it may, traces of this period can still be seen in some of the place names in the Rialto district. For example, we have the Traghetto del Buso (or "Hole") along the Grand Canal, the name of which, as Tassini wrote, is to be interpreted as "an obscene reference". Apparently, prostitutes arrived there on their way to their usual "walking spots" at Rialto when the Serenissima's laws against prostitution were waived. As some have pointed out, even the capitals flanking the doorway to Palazzo Camerlenghi, on the other side of the bridge, show a female figure with a flame burning between her legs and a male figure sporting a third, centrally-positioned, and rather large, "leg".

On the organisational-social level, however, the generalised concern about prostitution also led to provisions in favour of prostitutes, such as the founding of refuges for women wanting to leave "the trade" (the Ospedale del Soccorso, the Monastero delle Convertite and the Monastero delle Penitenti, for example), clinics for women with diseases associated with prostitution and also institutions that would take in girls who, because of their beauty or because of their family's impoverished state, might be forced into prostitution.

The Carampane area was once considered extremely dangerous for the casual visitor. Its tightly-knit houses, haphazardly-structured alleys, lack of lighting and social context made the area a sordid and dangerous area that was best avoided. Nowadays, however, the route from the spacious banks of the Grand Canal and Calle dei Boteri to Campiello Albrizzi and Campo San Polo is a fascination trip through what are perhaps the least artistically "gifted" areas of Venice but which nonetheless constitute a fascinating exercise in imagining the lifestyle of a very large slice of previous generations of Venetians.

16. Church of Sant'Aponal

The current church of Sant'Apollinare, popularly known as Sant'Aponal, was rebuilt according to the late-Gothic style in around 1550, and replaced the original 11th century church which had been destroyed by fire. The *campanile*, however, which had already been rebuilt in the Byzantine period, was not damaged and still maintains its original character. Above the little doorway there was once a marble representation of Byzantine lion, with closed book and undulating tail, one of the earliest representations of the Lion of St Mark, now in the Museo Correr. The interior of the church was reworked in the 16th century, and the church itself was suppressed in 1810 and its art works removed. It was bought in 1840, and an attempt was made to restore the original art works and re-consecrate the church. Of the eight altars it originally housed (one of which was almost certainly dedicated to the Scuola dei Tajapiera, or stonecutters, on the left-hand side of the church), only five were restored to their original form. During the 1929 restoration, an Istrian stone crucifix was installed above the large stained-glass rosette, and the main doorway was replaced (the original doorway was moved to the church of Sant'Elena, whence it had originally been taken in 1840) with a 14th century marble relief depicting scenes from the life of Christ. Unfortunately, the four large rectangular windows, which were added between 1810 and 1840 and have greatly altered the façade, were not removed. In the *campo*, just above the entrance to Sottoportico della Calle della Madonna, there is a small wooden panel which depicts the (unsubstantiated) story of Pope Alexander III who, fleeing from Barbarossa in 1177, arrived incognito in Venice and granted perpetual indulgence to anyone who said an Our Father and a Hail Mary on that very spot. Everybody seems to agree on the fact that Alexander III arrived incognito, but not everyone agrees on the spot itself. Many, in fact, maintain that it was the entrance to the church of San Salvador.

17. Church of San Giovanni Elemosinario

Anyone walking along Rialto's Ruga Vecchia San Giovanni, once called Ruga dei Oresi, would be forgiven for overlooking the church of San Giovanni Evangelista. In fact, its only entrance, a doorway on the Ruga, is hidden deep inside a vaulted, frescoed arch which is almost completely hidden by stalls. The church, which is also called the church of San Zuane de Rialto, was founded some time between the 9th and 10th centuries, and was destroyed by fire in 1180 and again in 1514. It was rebuilt by Scarpagnino in 1527-29, when it was given its current Greek cross form with Renaissance lines. The *campanile* itself collapsed, and was rebuilt in 1071 and again in 1361. The current, Gothic-like *campanile* lost its 1361 covering and small cupola, as well as its 15th century clock with bronze statues of two Moorish figures that would sound the bell each hour. As one of the greatest threats to Venice was fire, between 9 and 10 each evening a bell called the "Rialtina" would be rung from this *campanile*, warning Venetians that they had to put out all fires. Venice, in fact, was so obsessed with the fear of fire that glass blowing furnaces were all moved to Murano, for example, and a fire brigade was founded, and people also made use of symbolic and religious elements to ward off destruction by fire - stone crosses fixed to the façades of buildings and depictions of angels holding up coats-of-arms were added to the ground-floor entrance to *palazzi*, as well as other Renaissance images such as the salamander and the phoenix.

In 1519, the "Company of Venetian Couriers" were given their own altar in the church (their symbol has since been used the world over to indicate postal services). In the large entrance arch, copies of Marco Polo's *Il milione* and of the *Liber Albus* (a volume containing the main commercial treatises between Venice and other states) were made available for the local traders and merchants.

18. Campo di Rialto

On the San Polo side of Rialto Bridge, along Ruga dei Oresi (or Goldsmiths), there is the large Campo di Rialto (to your right as you look away from Rialto Bridge). The *campo* is surrounded on three sides by the Fabbriche Vecchie and, between the *campo* and Rialto Bridge, there is the church of San Giacometto. The Fabbriche were originally built at the very beginning of the Republican period but, after being destroyed by fire in 1514, they were rebuilt over a nine-year period by Scarpagnino. They continued to be called the Fabbriche *Vecchie* (or Old Factories) to distinguish them to the Fabbriche *Nuove* (or New Factories), built by Sansovino between 1552 and 1555 in the area between the Erbaria (or herb or vegetable market) and the Pescaria (or fish market). The great speed with which the area was rebuilt indicates just how important it was both functionally and economically for the city.

The church of San Giacometto, which was probably founded in 421, but official records first mention the church in the second half of the 13th century and state that it was consecrated in 1177. The church originally housed the altars for various *scuole*: that of the Oresi (who still now celebrate their annual feast day in the church), the Compravendi (sellers and buyers), the Casaroli (cheese vendors), the Travasadori de Olio (oil-merchants), the Biavaroli (grain vendors), the Garbeladori (grain selectors), the Ligadori de Comun (bale-makers) as well as the *scuole* for decorators, associations of boatsmen and bale-stampers. The church was not destroyed by the fire of 1514, and the many renovations it has undergone have left us an admirable church that is still used for normal religious services.

The Fabbriche Vecchie in the *campo* include the so-called Palazzo dei Dieci Savi (Ten Wise Men), the long building that goes from the bridge to Ruga Vecchia, and the buildings that delimit the *campo* and stretch down towards the Grand Canal, with a portico-ed structure used for stalls and shops and the two upper floors used for offices. The porticoes and *calli* are called BancoGiro (to the west, towards Palazzo dei Camerlenghi), della Sicurtà (the adjacent building) and Degli Oresi (towards Ruga Vecchia and along Palazzo dei Dieci Savi). The area was once a centre for insurance companies, and along with the more traditional agents linked with the Maritime Insurance Company (who defined contracts and interest rates – usually between 6 and 12% – on the basis of the routes and type and condition of the vessels insured), there were also "religious and business professionals" involved in insurance, with some very curious results. In 1587, for example, the Giudecca Convertite hospice stipulated an insurance contract with the Savi della Mercanzia, according to which the hospice would pray for the well-being of all insured vessels in return for 0.08% of the total sum for which the vessels had been insured. A special tribunal, whose job it was to decide on the validity of contracts, found the contract to be unacceptable, on the grounds that it was contrary to laws governing fair trade!

The ethics of commercial activity were very much to the fore, and various instruments and symbols were used to warn against potential unethical activity. For example, on the corner of Palazzo dei Dieci Savi there was a statue representing Justice, who was depicted not only with her usual scales but also wielding an enormous sword; just beneath the cross in the apse of the church there was an inscription that read "HOC CIRCA TEMPLUM SIT JUS MERCANTIBUS AEQUUM, PONDERA NEC VERGANT, NEC SIT CONVENTIO PRAVA" ("around this temple, may the law of the merchant and his weights be just and contracts be fair"); and the books *Liber Albus* and Marco Polo's *Il milione* were made available to local merchants and traders in the church of San Giovanni Elemosinario. Until the early 19th century, there was also a wooden pulpit in the *campo*, presumably also used to deliver sermons on the importance of honesty in mercantile life and other related themes.

19. The Herb and Fish Markets

The current layout of the area reflects the way in which, centuries ago, specific urban criteria were brought to bear in organising the herb and fish markets. The area closest to the Grand Canal is used for depositing goods and for bulk selling, while retail selling, from the largest goods to the smallest and most precious, takes place in the area that goes from the Grand Canal to the many stalls and shops in the main Rialto district. The administrative-commercial activities are all concentrated in the area around the market, in Campo di Rialto. The Erbaria, or herb and vegetable market, is contained within a triangle defined by Palazzo dei Camerlenghi, the Fabbriche Vecchie and Campo di Rialto and a part of the Fabbriche Nuove.

The large Calle Naranzaria (or Orangerie – used for moving shipments of citrus fruits) links the market area with Ruga degli Oresi. This is where the general retail market begins, with its cornucopia of fruit and vegetable stalls, distributed along Calle dei Oresi, Cordaria, Casaria, along the Fabbrica Nuova right up to Campo della Pescaria (or the fish market). Campo della Pescaria was paved as early as 1531, and was in part given over to fruit and vegetable stalls while the fishmongers occupied the shops on the ground floor of the nearby buildings. Fishmongers, in fact, are now mainly concentrated in the area that goes from Rio de le Becarie, under the porticoes of the 20th building (which was built in 1907, and bloodlessly reproduces late-Gothic Venetian architectural forms), right up to the buildings in Calle de le Becarie. It must be borne in mind that up to the end of the 18th century there were only 150 fishmongers (there were, at the same time, thousands of fishermen). This is explained by the fact that the only people allowed to sell fish were fishermen from the islands of San Nicolò and Poveglia who were at least 50 years old and had worked for at least 20. This was seen as a sort of reward for anyone who had suffered the hard lot reserved for fishermen of the period.

The part of the new building giving onto the Grand Canal is now used exclusively for the delivery of goods, as it is not generally thought appropriate for stalls. In fact, there is a little rhyme that can be heard in the markets about the new building: "massa alta i la gà fata, se se bagna col stravento, manco mal che semo in centro e no ne toca gnanca el sol" ("they've built it too high, and you get wet when it rains and the wind blows – thank God where here in the centre of town, and we don't even get a ray of sunshine").

Without in any way imposing on or overwhelming the original structure, there is a certain osmosis, born of necessity, between the various areas of Rialto; this is very likely the way things will remain, at least for as long as Venice maintains its own characteristics. The market area is always very interesting, whether you come during the day when activities are in full swing (and you are almost overwhelmed by the sheer flow of people and the noise of the sellers), or when the stalls are shut and the area is immersed in an almost unreal quiet that just begs you to sit down, relax and let your thoughts go.

All of these areas are imposingly towered over by the Fabbriche Vecchie and Nuove. The upper storeys of these buildings mainly housed, and continue to house, the law courts, almost as if, from way up on high, magistrates and judges wanted to reinforce their presence.

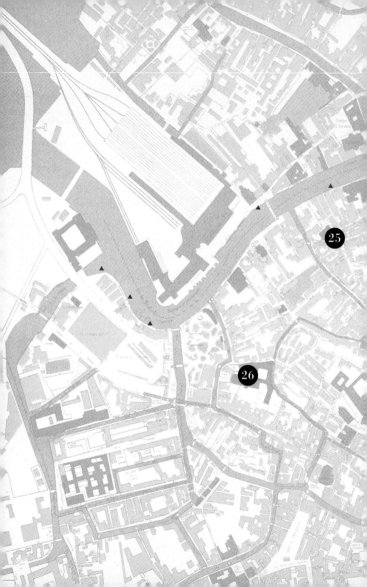

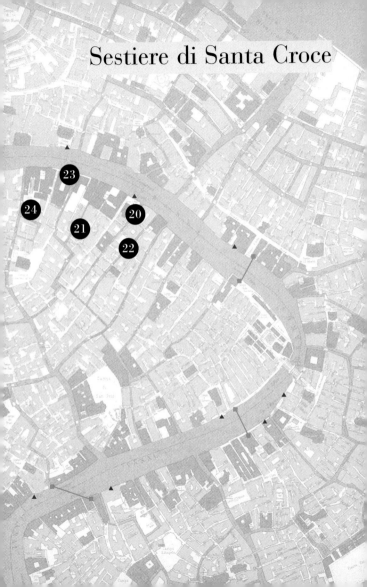

Sestiere di Santa Croce

20. Scoletta dei Tiraoro e dei Battiloro

"Scuola dell'Arte Tiraoro e Battioro" ("Tiraoro and Battioro School of Art"): this text can be found over the central section of the doorway to the little building next the church of San Stae (Sant'Eustachio) on the Grand Canal.

This is a unique building in Venice, and the man who was perhaps responsible for it was Gian Giacomo Gaspari, who had failed in his attempt to provide the winning project for the church of San Stae in 1709, but who was probably given the project for the more straightforward building next door, which was built in the same period. The two-storey building is characterised by superimposed curvilinear lines over the doorway, the windows and the upper part of the building and framing the central area which probably originally contained a painting.

The *scuola* was formed by two *"colonnelli"*, that is by two branches of art: the so-called *tiraoro* who worked gold into threads and wrapped it around a silk support, and the *battioro*, who beat gold leaf into extremely fine sheets that were placed between sheets of paper. Originally, only Venetians or Venetian citizens from the mainland were allowed to undertake the profession, although "foreigners" were later accepted. Even though the *scuola* worked gold, it was by no means a rich *scuola*. In fact, its chronic shortage of funds and its mounting debts were so alarming that in 1807, when the notary Jacopo Delfini and the commissioner Antonio Novello handed the *scuola* over to the public domain after the Napoleonic suppression of all Venetian *scuole*, it was found that the *scuola* had only 132 Veneto lire to its credit, and owed 9,300.

The building was subsequently sold to Angela Barbarigo, and on her death it was inherited by the clergy, who used it as a coal deposit. It was then bought by Antonio Correr in 1876, who transformed it into an art gallery. The building is still used as such.

21. Casa Agnusdio

With Ca' Pesaro behind you, as you walk down Fondamenta Ca' Pesaro, you will see a late 14th century building on the other side of the canal. The building is known as Casa Agnusdio (Lamb of God), and, compared to the imposing monumentality of Ca' Pesaro, it seems much more like a common town house than a *palazzo*. But what is so fascinating about it is the fullness and beauty of its stone ornamentation – the frieze over the doorway on Ponte Forner, the pentaforate window, the entrance from the canal surmounted by a patera with a Lamb of God and moulding. 13th century Romanesque friezes have been added to the arched lintel around the doorway, as if to delimit the field within which three proto-14th century angels hold aloft a noble coat-of-arms. The pentaforate window is a precious masterpiece, most probably undertaken by an architect stonemason. It is obviously mid-14th century Gothic, and six reliefs depicting evangelical symbols and the Annunciation fill the spaces and balance out the inflexions of the arches, which are surrounded by a check frame and based on archaic capitals with diamond-point friezes. The boat entrance is a simple split arch on a Gothic check frame moulded from within, surmounted by a patera depicting the mystical lamb.

Stonework such as this can sometimes be found unexpectedly in the *calli* (there is also a beautiful doorway in Calle del Tiozzi in front of Ponte del Forner), where the buildings and tightly-knit streets often hide them from visitors until the very last moment. But when you do come across them, your main thought is that there must be so much that has yet to be explored amongst the "minor" art and architecture of Venice, which in the past was famous both for the quantity and quality of its decorative elements.

22. Campo Santa Maria Mater Domini

As you enter Campo Santa Maria Domini over the bridge bearing the same name, to your left you will see the old 13th century houses that belonged to the Zane family and characterised by the overhanging roof and a Veneto-Byzantine quadriforate window with chains and crosses. To the right, you can see the acute-arched 14th century Casa Barbaro and, in the background, Palazzetto Viaro-Zane, with its Gothic first floor (including a 14th century pentaforate window), its Renaissance second and third floors and Renaissance courtyard and interior staircase. The central plaque of the pentaforate window once contained a small lion (included in 1797 by order of Napoleon), indicating those houses that had been confiscated from families that had taken part in the Bajamonte Tiepolo plot in 1310.

If compared to the typical scheme for rectangular *campi*, Santa Maria Mater Domini's church is shifted slightly to the right of the main axis. This was probably due to the fact that there was originally a series of buildings belonging to the Monastero di Santa Cristina, to which the church was attached. The current church is situated in the same spot where the original church was built in 960. This original church was later rebuilt several times. The last reconstruction, in the current Renaissance form, dates from 1503. Giovanni Buora and Mauro Codussi are given as its probable authors, with Sansovino working on the façade. The current *campanile* was rebuilt in 1743, on the same spot as the previous one, which had collapsed in 1740. Originally, the *campanile* could be reached from the Campo via a little portico, but the Council of Ten issued a decree in 1488, demanding that access to the *campanile* be closed off with a wooden gate: they were worried that the *campanile* had become a "meeting-place, especially at night, for sodomites and other dishonest persons". The rest of the wooden sections of the *sottoportico* held up by three pillars with capitals can still be seen inside the church.

23. Fondaco del Megio

This large, restrained construction on the Grand Canal, probably dating from the 14th century, is still virtually as it was when Jacopo de' Barbari originally built it. The only modification is the 20th century reworking of the Lion of St Mark, undertaken by the sculptor Carlo Lorenzetti, replacing the original lion which had been added after the fall of the Republic. The building's large warehouse space and its large protective wall, its lack of a portico and other functional structures, as well as its position, all indicate that, unlike other *fonteghi*, this building was not intended to be used for the storage of foodstuffs for the general population. For this there were the San Silvestro and St Mark's granaries (the former in Rialto, the latter in the area currently occupied by the Giardinetti Reali), which were also used for milling grain; they were also more strategically placed in the busier parts of the city. Fondaco del Megio was therefore used for storing those grain supplies that would probably be needed for military or emergency reasons (wars and food shortages, for example), and was consequently situated where it could most readily be reached by large vessels but not by people in general. There were not many such emergency situations in Venice's history, and the only ones officially mentioned are those of 1346, 1527, 1559 and 1570. Doge Pietro Loredan, who ordered that the Fondaco del Megio's grain supplies should be used in 1570 for the production of bread, was given the nickname of "el doge megioto" ("the Grain Doge"), and even though it was clear that thanks to his edict many Venetians were saved from certain starvation, the following was reported to have been shouted at his funeral: "the Grain Doge, who made bakers sell bread made from the Megio supplies, is dead! Long live St Mark and the Nobility, for the Famine Doge is dead!" The large warehouse has now been turned into a primary school, but the extant, and rather plain, façade and the nearby places still serve to conserve its memory.

24. Campo San Zan Degolà

The island facing the Grand Canal between Rio del Fontego and Rio di San Zan Degolà (St John the Beheaded) is elongated and rather less wide at its centre. The area between the Grand Canal and the centre of the island has Campo San Zan Degolà at its heart. The *campo* is rather small, and is in one of the quietest areas of the city, where the buildings have for the most part maintained their characteristic features, volumes and architectural forms. Very recent restoration work has only eliminated the sense of desolation that the *campo* once had, especially when it was still covered in weeds. The few historical references to the *campo* are perfectly in keeping with its very retired and perhaps even slightly wild appearance. It was, for example, once inhabited by Biasio (whose name was then bestowed on the nearby bank of the Grand Canal), who killed children and then stewed them for dinner, and whose punishment was as cruel as his crimes.

The Campo is dominated by the church of the same name, which was founded in 1007. It has been constantly restored, the most important restorations taking place in the 16th century and 1703, when it was completely restructured. The church is the only example from which we can deduce tangible evidence about the size and structure of the many Veneto-Byzantine buildings that have since been so modified that their original form has been completely lost. The interior is of the Gothic basilica type and there are still remains of 12th-13th century Byzantine frescoes.

Because of the church's modest size, the Doges could not use the church to celebrate the anniversary of Venice's victorious battle against Genoa, which had taken place on the feast day of St John the Baptist. The anniversary was therefore celebrated at St Mark's.

Beyond the *rio* there is the 17th century Palazzo Gidoni, with its triforate window and doorway surmounted by tympana.

25. Church of San Simeon Grando

The church of San Simeone Profeta (St Simon the Prophet) is popularly referred to as San Simeon Grando to distinguish it from the church of Santi Simeone and Giuda Apostoli (St Simon and Jude the Apostles), which is called the church of San Simeon Piccolo. The adjectives of "grande" and "piccolo" ("large" and "small", respectively) are used in their old sense, and Jacopo de' Barbari's plan, in fact, depicts San Simeon Piccolo as much smaller than the other church, albeit totally different from the current one. The church of San Simeon Grando, however, appears to be situated in the same place and to be of the same size as the church currently in the *campo*, even though the original roof structure was presumably different, based as it was on the basilica type with three naves. It probably had a low roof that jutted out along the entire width of the façade. The current building, which is in fact Domenico Margutti's 18th century reconstruction, is smaller than the original. Under the portico of the residences near the church, there is beautiful stele that is popularly referred to as "San Simeon no me ne impasso" ("St Simon I couldn't care less") because of position of the saint's hands. This stele is, in fact, a 14th century representation of St Ermolao, whose body was brought back to Venice in 1205, and which is currently held in the church once used by members of the St Ermolao confraternity. Margutti's original renovation was followed by further restoration work undertaken by Massari, who created a new façade in 1755. Further restoration work carried out in 1861 led to the discovery of an older floor with burial seals (it had originally been covered in 1630, when a magistrate ordered that the floor be covered by another floor after a man who had died from the plague had been buried there); the same restoration, however, also removed all remaining traces of the 18th century work on the building and façade.

26. Church of the Tolentini

Building began on the church of the Tolentini in 1591 on the site of a prior oratory dedicated to San Nicolò da Tolentino, annexed to the parish of San Pantalon. The Theatine brothers commissioned Scamozzi to draw up the plans, apparently according to a model that Palladio himself had partially overseen. The immense Corinthian pronaos on the façade was built between 1706 and 1714 according to a design by Andrea Tirali. The convent annexed to the church was built in the same period. The convent was gradually enlarged with the addition of dormitories, gardens, cloister, library, refectory and orchards.

Scamozzi did not complete the project, perhaps because of the excessive costs involved and the building methods, which the brothers were rather wary of. Rumour was rife in Venice about the affair, as Scamozzi often complained about the brothers' treatment to the stonemason Melchisedech (Baldassarre Longhena's father) in his workshop, which was frequented by Venetian artists. The building was nonetheless completed according to the original plans, and was consecrated on October 20th, 1602, and dedicated to San Nicolò da Tolentini. The interior contains a single wide nave with three side chapels. There was originally a cupola over the transept, of which only the tambour remained when, for safety reasons, the cupola was dismantled in the 18th century.

The grandiosity of the bank in front of Campo dei Tolentini is due to the fact that the Doges and Venetian nobility would visit the site to thank St Gaetano for having helped Venice win the war, begun of the feast day of St Gaetano, that led to the conquest of Corinth and Athens.

In 1810, the complex was turned into a barracks and the church was demoted to a parish church. It currently houses the Faculty of Architecture, and the entrance is now along the side flank of the building, via a cement doorway that was designed by the architect Carlo Scarpa in 1985.

27. Church of San Pantalon

The current church of San Pantalon was built on the same ground that its predecessor occupied, even though it was turned 90 degrees in order to realign the façade and main entrance with the *campo*. The original church emphasised the side entrance onto the *campo*, while the main entrance gave onto the *rio*, as can be evinced from Jacopo de' Barbari's plan (1500). The first building is attested to indirectly in the 10th century, where the church is said to have been rebuilt in 1009. Its façade gave onto Rio delle Mosche and the *campanile* flanked the side of the church on the *campo* side. In 1222 the church was restored, and in 1305 it was consecrated by the Bishop of Castello, Ramperto Polo, the same man who was later killed by his parishioners on Fondamenta del Malcanton. In the second half of the 17th century, the church was deemed unstable and demolished, only to be rebuilt in the 18th century according to a project by F Comino (the church was given its current form and orientation); the *campanile*, however, was reconstructed by Giovanni Antonio Scalfarotto. The façade was never finished. Inside the church there is a remarkable ceiling painting, the largest of its kind, that Gian Antonio Fiumani (also buried in the church) took almost thirty years to complete.

St Pantaleon, who was the Emperor Galerius' doctor, was beheaded in 305 after having been denounced by his colleagues during Diocletian's persecution of Christians. In the Middle Ages he was considered the patron saint of doctors. "Pantalon" seems to have derived from the saint's name, and as a term has been used to refer to Venetians in general; it is less likely that "Pantalon" derived from the expression "*pianta leoni*" ("lion planters"), used to describe Venetians' planting their flag, depicting a lion, whenever they conquered a country or city. There is as yet no consensus on whether the name of the Venetian masque, Pantalon, derived from the name used to describe Venetians, or vice versa.

28. Campo Santa Margherita

Campo Santa Margherita's current form dates from 1845, when part of the San Barnaba canal was filled in. The original canal ran through the southern end of the Campo and then wound its way back to San Barnaba near the Ponte delle Pazienze. The section of canal that flowed through the Campo was originally called Rio della Scoazzera (i.e. "rubbish") because refuse would be stacked up on the banks of the Rio, and this probably explains why the larger buildings were built at the opposite end of the Campo. The Campo was originally similar in structure to the nearby Campo San Pantalon, that is with the church placed on a transversal axis in the northern end of the Campo, the *campanile* on the Campo side of the church and the side entrance to the church architecturally embellished. In the first half of the 17th century, the original church was in such poor shape that it was completely rebuilt following a plan by the painter Giovanni Battista Lambranzi. Along the side facing San Pantalon, the façade of the parish priest's residence was decorated and the windows were given Baroque stone frames and gargoyles holding up the eaves, which continue right round to the right-hand side of the façade.

In 1805, the church was not amongst those listed in a Napoleonic decree which forced 32 of Venice's 40 parish church's to close. It did not fare quite so well in 1810, however, when another decree put an end to virtually all religious activity in the city (the *campanile* had already been demolished in 1808 for safety reasons). After the 1810 decree, the church's furnishings and altars were removed and the church was used for non-religious functions (it is currently used as an auditorium by the local university). The isolated building in the middle of the Campo dates back to 1725. It was once the Scuola dei Varoteri (or tanners) and dedicated to the Visitation; it was also a faithful reconstruction of the *scuola* that had been demolished in Campo dei Gesuiti.

29. Campo San Barnaba

The area of San Barnaba, which gives onto the Grand Canal and is delimited by Rio San Barnaba and Rio Malpaga, dates from the 9th century. The buildings have been laid out according to a scheme which was typical for rectangularly-shaped islands: transversal residential buildings, with interposed alleys and a linking *calle* cutting across the little alleys and running the length of the buildings. The current church was last renovated by Boschetti in the 18th century. The *campanile* has largely retained its original structure, with the simple addition of the pinnacle in the 14th century. The houses around the Campo are mainly from the 16th-18th centuries. If you come to San Barnaba from Campo Santa Margherita along Rio Terà Canal (see chapter 29), you will cross Ponte dei Pugni, where there are four footprints in white stone. The bridge was once used for ferocious battles between the two warring Venetian factions of the "Castellani" and "Nicolotti". The former were from the eastern end of the city, and wore a red beret and scarf; the latter were from the western part, and wore a black beret and scarf. Amongst the preordained occasions for battle between the two there was the so-called Battle of the Fists, or Pugni, during which the two opposing factions could engage in battle on various bridges between September and Christmas. One of the most popular bridges was, in fact, Ponte dei Pugni, which originally had no railing. There were three types of battle: the *mostra*, (two "champions" would fight it out on a bridge, and the winner was the one who managed to keep out of the water); the *frota* (the two factions would clash, and any form of attack or defence was allowed); and the *guerra ordinata* (one of the two factions would "conquer" a bridge, but only pushing and shoving were allowed). The battles were outlawed in 1705 because of the large numbers of people hurt and because of the riots they gave rise to. They were substituted by organised competitions, known as *Le forze di Ercole* ("The feats of Hercules"), and regattas.

30. Palazzo Ariani

Palazzo Ariani was built at the point where Rio San Basegio, Rio dei Carmini and Rio dell'Anzolo Rafael meet. It takes its name from the family who had owned practically all of the Angelo Raffaele area since the 9th century.

In the second half of the 14th century, the *palazzo* was rebuilt according to its current form, with the hexalobate windows surmounted by a double row of quadrilobate windows, with trilobate windows between the arches, defined by torus moulding (recalling similar examples in the Doge's Palace). These characteristics, along with the motif on the beehive fretwork, hark back to the French Gothic more than the English, with some oriental influences. The structure of and solutions for the portico on the ground floor (which begins with a wooden architrave holding up the corner of the façade), the lateral staircase, the side windows (amongst the first to use inflected trilobate arches) and the window jambs below intended to continue the supporting corbels for the little terrace with a roughly-hewn balustrade all lead us to the conclusion that this rather rudimentary building was perhaps the work of an architect-stonemason who had not artistically "matured" in the city. Nonetheless, it is still a building with a well-defined place in 14th century Venetian architecture and which gives some indication of the development that Gothic window ornamentation would subsequently undergo in the 15th century.

The two carved shields in the central panels of the parapet of the hexalobate are clearly of the Ariani family. When the family died out in 1650 the building went to the Pasqualigo family, and then, in 1769, to the Pasinetti brothers (Antonio and Carlo) and finally, after part of the building had been sold to a member of the Cicogna family, it was donated to the city of Venice in 1849, since when the building has been used as a school.

31. Church of San Nicolò dei Mendicoli

According to tradition, the church was founded in the 7th century by a group of Paduans fleeing from the Longobards. The small island of San Nicolò was once called the Mendigola (or "mendicant") because of the abject poverty of its inhabitants. These were mainly fishermen, and were considered short-tempered and proud of their poverty. They constituted a community which was allowed a certain amount of autonomy, and had their own fishing customs. They also had their own *gastaldo* (or "steward"), called "the Doge of the Nicolotti", who was elected annually by the islanders and was received by the Doge of Venice in his Palace. They were the backbone of the "Nicolotti" faction of Venice (the other being the "Castellani" – see chapter 29).

The church was reconstructed in the 13th century and, although it has often been restored, it has managed to maintain its original plan, mainly because the island never quite had enough money for renovations. The more important interventions were the addition of a portico in the 15th century (which was used as a nocturnal refuge by the *pizochere*, that is "penitent women" or ex-prostitutes), a complete restructuring in 1580 (the church was provided with a new iconostasis and the walls and ceiling were covered in gilded wood, paintings and statues similar to those in the Carmini), the Istrian stone side façade and the altar in the third chapel on the right (all dating from the 1850s). When the altar was added, however, gossip in the area led the local judge to investigate into how the commissioner, Brother Giovanni Zaniol, had come by the large amount of money needed for the altar. According to Cicogna, the brother had found large amounts of gold and silver inside one of the tombs in the *campanile*; Zaniol, however, never let on.

Beside the church there are a 13th century Veneto-Byzantine *campanile* and the San Filippo Neri oratory, with its 18th century doorway topped by a blind window and stone frame.

32. Church of San Raffaele

Tradition has it that the church was founded in 640, and some even maintain that it was founded as early as 416. If we consider the general context, and if we also bear in mind that churches were used not only for religious purposes but that they also played a social-organisational role, and that, in the 9th century, Venice was quickly becoming a large city, then neither of these dates would seem at all far-fetched. However, the church is first mentioned in an official document in 1193, where reference is made to the fact that a new church, replacing the original building which had burnt down in 1149, had been consecrated. The current building was reconstructed by the architect Contino (Francesco Contin) in the first half of the 17th century. The façade dates from 1736-49, and was added to replace the original façade, which had collapsed during restoration work. At the same time, the organ (with decorations by Francesco Guardi on the parapet) was also added, just behind the façade inside the church. Two façades, similar to the main façade facing the canal, were added along the side walls. Nothing was added to the apse wall, however, and the exterior was not completed because of funding problems. Despite the addition of a small building, the *campo* behind the church, which contains both the church of Angelo Raffaele and the church of San Sebastiano, is still a beautiful, comfortably ensconced space. Due to a shortage of funds, the very modest nature of the changes made to the area and the filling in of the little *rio* that flows alongside San Sebastiano and the *campo* have conferred on the complex a strange, almost "edge-of-town" feel – the area seems to emanate an oddly strange aura somewhere between retiring privacy and abandonment, and the two churches, whose apses give onto the campo, seem to have turned their back on each other.

33. Church of San Sebastiano

A first church dedicated to St Sebastian was erected in the area just beside the current church between 1455 and 1468. It was a Gothic structure, and was destroyed only a few decades later. The current, Renaissance church was built between 1505 and 1548 by Scarpagnino. The façade is covered in marble and the right-hand side has been given large oval windows just under the eaves and a semicircular stone portico over the side entrance. The *campanile* dates from the same period, even though the conic pinnacle (covered in small polychrome brickwork) with octagonal drum was added later.

The church, however, is fascinating because of the way Scarpagnino changed the volumetric structures within and because of its exceptional decorations. The plan is that of a Latin cross, with a single nave, a plain ceiling and an atrium with hanging chancel which extends along either side over the three side chapels. The presbytery with cupola and apses is flanked by two small chapels. The left chapel has a majolica floor (1510) with singular designs and patterns.

A pictorial cycle by Veronese (1528-1588) occupies the church and sacristy. As Lorenzetti says, the cycle (a mixture of oil painting and fresco) is a *summa* of "the principles, the technique and the sublime nature" of the artist. Tradition has it that Veronese was exiled here for some time, either for having killed a man who had insulted him or because he had offended an important personage, but there is no documented proof for either of these assertions. Veronese was buried in the church, which contains what is perhaps his greatest work.

34. San Trovaso

"Trovaso" is a contraction of the names of Saints Gervasio and Protasio. "San Trovaso" refers not only to the church, but also the *campo*, the *rio*, the bridge and the *squero*. The entire complex is light and spacious, and leads to the Zattere. The *rio* is not only a very important water-way between the Grand Canal and Giudecca Canal; on either side, there are also two wide paths on either side of the *rio*, thus demonstrating that, in Venice, the water-ways are used principally for transport while the "land" routes are used by people. After Ponte di San Trovaso, near the Zattere, the canal gets progressively wider, and eventually leads to a complex *campo*, where the church and other buildings (and especially the *squero*) divide the area into a series of smaller, asymmetrical and interconnected sections which have been put to different uses and functions. In Campo San Trovaso proper, the main façade of the church is parallel to Rio Ognissanti and flanked by two wings of low houses. In front of the church there is a well, with the entire water-collecting area raised in order to increase the surface area for the collection of water (at the same time, salty flood waters cannot infiltrate into the well). The right-hand side of the church gives onto Rio San Trovaso, and there is a large area, almost a second *campo*, between it and the *rio*, bearing witness to the importance given to the water-way. This little *campo* also has its own well. This perhaps explains why the church has been given a second façade, similar to the main one, which is also flanked by two wings of low houses and the *campanile*.

The original project for the church was by Palladio, and it was built in the late 16th century. Like Angelo Raffaele, tradition has it that the original church on the site was founded in the first half of the 9th century, which was followed by reconstructions in 1028, 1105 and 1585. Each reconstruction was probably undertaken for safety reasons, save the 1105 one, which was due to the church being destroyed by the great fire that, in fact, destroyed much of Venice. On the corner between Rio San Trovaso and Rio Ognissanti, there are a series of low wooden houses huddled around a plot of land that slopes down towards the water: this is the San Trovaso *squero*, the oldest of the few that are still in operation in contemporary Venice. There were once hundreds of *squeri* in the city, all either building or repairing boats, and were the equivalent of modern garages in our own metropolises. The word "*squero*" does not, as some maintain, derive from "*squarda*" (or team), but from *eschàrion*, a Greek term that referred to an upturned trestle, used for the boats being worked on. The *squeraroli*, that is the workers in the *squero*, had their own Scuola, which was also open to the *peateri*, (i.e., those who built *peate*, large boats very similar to barges, which are now hardly ever used). The Scuola had its altar in the church of San Trovaso. This *squero*, which dates back to the 17th century, is made up of three mainly wooden buildings. The larger two are actually residences, while the lower, longer building, with roof and wet-dock, is used for repairing and building boats. It is in the "Cadore" style, which is not surprising considering that the first owners were from Cadore, a city which also provided the wood used in both the smaller craft and the galleys and galleons originally made in the Serenissima. The San Trovaso *squero* is now mainly used exclusively for the construction and maintenance of gondolas, the "queen" of rowing craft used to transport people. According to Sansovino, there were about 10,000 gondolas in Venice in 1500; according to Moretti, there were about 1,475 in 1760. Now there are only about 500.

Gondolas are still being built using traditional methods, and still conform to traditional size: they are 10.835 metres long, 1.42 metres wide at their widest point, and weigh 350 kilos. They are made up of 280 parts, and seven different types of wood are used. It is perfectly balanced and makes no noise as it moves through the water. It leans slightly to the right, and is also slightly asymmetrical so as to perfectly counteract the rower's thrusts. Since 1633, all gondolas are black, including the removable cabin, or *felze*, which has now almost completely disappeared.

35. Campiello Barbaro

 Ponte San Cristoforo is one of the most characteristic of Venice, and one of the most beautiful, with the elegant curve of its parapet, the quarter-turn staircase and the marble decorations in the top corner. The *rio* is so small and the second flight of steps so well-disguised that it looks less like a bridge than a flight of stairs joining two distinct urban spaces. With the simple addition of a couple of tables, wrought-iron chairs and a bistro, you would be forgiven for thinking you were in Paris. Palazzo Dario was built in 1487, based on a project by Pietro Lombardo and his collaborators, for Giovanni Dario, a *bailo* (or Venetian Ambassador) to Constantinople and who ratified a peace treaty with the Turks in 1479. Not long after it was built, it was passed on to the Barbaro family, who also owned the *palazzo* next door on the Grand Canal and gave their name to the little *campo* and *calle*. The *palazzo*, however, is believed to bestow bad luck on its owners, and considering the tragedies that have befallen most of them it is hard not to believe this. Giovanni Dario's daughter, for whom the *palazzo* was originally built, came to an untimely and grizzly end; her husband was disqualified from the Maggior Consiglio; and the building's last owner, Raul Gardini, took his own life in the *palazzo*. The history of its inhabitants is more than enough to add a sinister glow to the light that reflects off the beautiful multi-coloured façade at sunset and to evoke sinister figures standing at the leaded windows in otherwise sumptuous rooms. Many of its owners, however, had very good luck (which is never quite as memorable as its opposite, and certainly isn't the stuff that popular lore is made of). One such case is recalled by the plaque in Campiello Barbaro, which contains a text dictated by the poet Diego Valeri: *"In questa casa antica dei Dario, Henri de Régnier – poeta di Francia – venezianamente visse e scrisse – anni 1899-1911"* ("In this ancient house of the Dario family, Henri de Régnier – poet of France – lived and wrote Venetian-ly – 1899-1911").

36. Le Zitelle, Giudecca

The real name of the Zitelle hospice is "Ospizio di Santa Maria della Presentazione" ("The Hospice of the Holy Virgin of the Presentation"). It was founded by Benedetto Palmio, a Jesuit priest, in 1561, the same year work began on a building with annexed oratorio on the Giudecca, designed by Palladio.

The term *"ospizio"* in Venetian had different meanings: it was sometimes used to describe areas that were used to quarantine individuals or groups of people, a hospital especially for people with contagious diseases; it was sometimes a refuge or a school, and sometimes offered living quarters for young people, especially young women from impoverished families. Over time, even though they maintained their charitable nature, these hospices began to specialise in cultural and educational, and especially musical, areas.

The Zitelle hospice was founded "in order to give succour to and educate all those poor young women who, because of their beauty, might otherwise be tempted to compromise their virtue". The hospice therefore took in *zitelle*, or poor young women, and looked after them until they were old enough to marry. Their education included domestic skills, such as embroidery (and especially "raised point embroidery", for which the hospice became famous), and singing.

The hospice's church was built between 1582 and 1586 by Jacopo Bozzetto (based on a project by Palladio, who died two years before building began). Music, in fact, was so important to the hospice that the building was specially designed to enhance the acoustics.

The wings of the hospice branch out from the central church, and are aligned with the façade. An ideal line drawn from the lantern of the cupola and following sloping line of the roof would give as a pyramidal shape. A transversal body joins the wings and surrounds the apse, thus constituting a central, porticoed wall. A further two walls delimit the little cloister behind the building, which opens out onto the lagoon.

Building on the Giudecca has mainly been undertaken on the northern side, with the fields, gardens and orchards on the southern side. If you observe the Giudecca from the Zattere, the long island seems to have been specially designed as a scenic break to an otherwise drab and repetitive horizon.

Older names for the Giudecca have an oddly archaic feel to them: "Spinale" and "Spina Laguna" (i.e. "fish-bone" and "Lagoon fish-bone" respectively, perhaps because of the shape of the island), which was separated from Venice by "Vigano" or "Carbonario" ("street" and "coal-works", so-called because it separated a small town and because coal-bearing barges would use the strip of water).

The current name, however, perhaps derives from the island's original Jewish residents, who had two synagogues (now destroyed) and who left behind a recently-discovered slab of stone with Hebrew inscriptions (found near the Zitelle hospice). Another hypothesis is that the name might derive from the Venetian word *zudegà* (adjudged), a term used in the 9th century to describe the sentence by which judges gave land on the Giudecca to families of rebels who had been banned from the city of Venice.

The island is actually made up of eight smaller islands which are linked by a series of bridges, and is a maze of little *rii* and *calli*. There is only one *fondamenta*, on the side of the island looking towards Venice, and a wing of houses that is punctuated by the cupolas of the Zitelle hospice and the Redentore church, between the moorings in front of Mulino Stucky to the right, and the island of San Giorgio to the left. On the lagoon side of the island there are a series of orchards and vegetable gardens, which very few have had the occasion to visit.

The Zitelle hospice now no longer takes in young impoverished women, but its premises are still used for cultural and musical events.

37. Rio Terà dei Catecumeni

Rio Terà dei Catecumeni can be found on the Zattere, just beyond Ponte di Ca' Balà at the end of the Magazzini del Sale (built by the architect Pigazzi in the 19th century). This area's original rarefied and abstract character of almost total solitude was ruined in the 19th century when Rio dei Saloni and Rio dei Catecumeni were filled in. There was no real reason for tampering with the perfectly integrated mix of walkways and waterways, which should have been maintained both for aesthetic and functional reasons.

As you walk along Rio Terà dei Catecumeni, you can see Casa Costantini to your left. This is a composite building, with Gothic and 16th century windows, and an architrave portico with *barbacani*.

Further along, to your right, there is the Ospizio Catecumeni, which the architect Giorgio Massari was commissioned to build in 1727. The name and function of the building hark back centuries, to the period in which many prisoners and slaves were brought to Venice from the East, to be used to do the humbler jobs that Venetians refused to accept. In 1517, the Serenissima set up a refuge for those who had more or less integrated into local society, and who were willing to convert to Christianity. The "*catecumeni*", as they were called, were first put up in a house at San Marcuola, then Santi Appostoli. With the arrival of even more prisoners after the Battle of Lepanto (1571), the number of *catecumeni* became so large that a whole group of houses had to be found for them (this site was where Madonna della Salute currently stands). In 1727, it was finally decided that a whole, much larger complex would be built. This complex consists of living quarters built around an oratory, a courtyard and small cloister, according to a project that was later used by Palladio for the Zitelle, and Scamozzi for his Ospizio dei Mendicanti.

The façade for the oratory, dedicated to St John the Baptist but simply called "I Catecumeni", is simple despite its compositional elements, and is completely closed off by the façade of the hospice itself, which is much higher. The larger façade was made as simple as possible so as not to detract from the church itself. The complex is currently run by the an order of nuns, and is used as a kindergarten, primary school and lodgings for university students.

38. Abbey of San Gregorio

In the late Middle Ages, Benedictine abbeys were fulcrums around which life in general and cultural tradition in particular were brought together. Many such convents were built, both in the centre of Venice and on the outskirts of the city, between the 9th to the 12th centuries. The San Gregorio Abbey is part of the buildings that the Benedictines had built in the lagoon area and that included about 35 different sites, of which 13 in the city of Venice itself. The San Gregorio convent was part of the larger abbey of Sant'Illario, which had been founded in the 9th century and constituted one of the oldest Benedictine settlements in the Veneto. Up to the 15th century, the main headquarters were at the mouth of the River Brenta, where water and land traffic to and from Padua could be kept under control. When the Benedictines abandoned their mainland headquarters, they moved to the San Gregorio convent. This convent basically had a very tall Gothic church and a lower monastery which was built around two cloisters along the Grand Canal, right up to Rio della Salute and Calle del Traghetto. The current church is a reconstruction undertaken in 1445-1461. Like the preceding church, it is characteristically Gothic, and, until the last century, it also had a façade with pinnacle arches and stone niches topped with statues. The few elements that are still extant, the rosette, doorway, windows and apses, are well-conserved. The façade now gives onto a typical *campiello*, whose elements have been modified, albeit without compromising its authentic nature. The convent was also rebuilt in the 15th century. Its original characteristics, however, have been conserved in the main doorway on the Grand Canal, the niche and side windows, the first of the two cloisters and, despite the addition of large windows, even the sides giving onto the Grand Canal and Campo della Salute. Like many others, the complex lost its original religious function in 1805. It is currently owned by the Venice City Council, and houses the Centro del Restauro of the Veneto Government Office for Art Galleries and Works of Art.

39. Madonna della Salute

Each year on November 21st (feast day of the Presentation of the Virgin Mary, even though for Venetians it is the feast day of the Madonna of the Salute) Venice celebrates the end of the 1636 Plague. It is the most popular feast in the city, and is the only one that has maintained its original religious character. A votive bridge of barges goes from Campo Santa Maria del Giglio to the church of the Salute, and is thronged with processions and a constant flow of the religious faithful. Campo della Salute and the surrounding area are full of stalls selling votive candles of all sizes and typically Venetian sweets. The sheer numbers of people take us back to an older Venice when people were profoundly devout, and you can still feel a certain nostalgia for the days of the Serenissima.

According to historians, the plague arrived in Western Europe in the early 14th century, and in Venice in 1348, when about half the population died. The second Plague arrived in 1575-77, and the third and last Plague in 1630-31. In the city of Venice alone, about 25% of the 180,000 inhabitants died during the second Plague, and about 30% of the 143,000 inhabitants during the third. The Plague, however, never completely disappeared between these dates – it flared up at irregular intervals, and its consequences were no less tragic for being less marked. Strigis, an ambassador for the Duke of Mantua to the Emperor's court, died on June 8th, 1630, and is considered the first victim of the 1630-31 Plague. The disease was first noted during the summer and winter months, but the full impact was felt during the early months of 1631. Venice cut off all activities with the outside world, and severe measures were taken to ward off the worst effects of the plague: houses, and sometimes entire blocks of buildings, were sequestered, anything that plague victims had come into contact with was burnt, people were quarantined in the lagoon's *lazzaretti* (the name, later used in other languages to denote quarantine quarters, derives from the island of Lazzaretto the Elder, where anyone suspected of being plague-ridden was dispatched: the name was itself a corruption of the name "Santa Maria di Nazareth", hence *nazaretum* and eventually *lazzaretto*). Nothing was left to chance: even correspondence was handled exclusively with a special prong with large, flat blades and nails, which punched little holes into the letters which were then disinfected using special scents and vapours. Bearing in mind that the end of the 1576 Plague had led to the votive building of the Redentore, on October 22nd the Senate decreed that "His Most Serene Prince publicly maketh a solemn vow to His Divine Majesty to erect in this city a Church bearing the name of the Holy Virgin, the which shall be dedicated to the Holy Mother of Succour [*Salute*]; and each twelve-month on the day that this city shall be declared free of the present pestilence, His Serenity and all His successors shall solemnly go forth with the entire Senate and pay homage at the self-same church in perpetual memory of the public gratitude for the city's deliverance". On March 25th, 1631, Doge Nicolò Contarini, accompanied by the Patriarch Giovanni Tiepolo, laid the first stone on the site of the Madonna della Salute. The date was chosen as it was the feast day of the Annunciation, but also because it was the day on which Venice itself had been founded. This explains the floor inscription that can be found in the church: "UNDE ORIGO, INDE SALUS 1631" ("From our origins, unto health 1631"). The definitive project for the church had yet to be chosen. Of the 11 projects, two were shortlisted by the commission: a traditional, Latin-cross plan by Antonio Smeraldi; and a central plan by Baldassarre Longhena. The latter was eventually declared the winner, not only because of its exceptional quality but also because as novel a construction as Longhena's was considered to be emblematic of a great challenge, and was rightly seen to be perfectly in keeping with the other buildings between San Giorgio and the city. The church is underpinned by 1,156,627 wooden poles, used to reclaim and reinforce the land on which the church was built. The church took 50 years to complete, and Longhena just managed to see his masterpiece completed before he died in 1682. The church was consecrated five years later. From the top of the steps you can see the white-on-grey decorations that Longhena designed for the pavement of Campo della Salute, and through the November mist you can only just make out, beyond the Grand Canal, the outlines of St Mark's and the Doge's Palace.

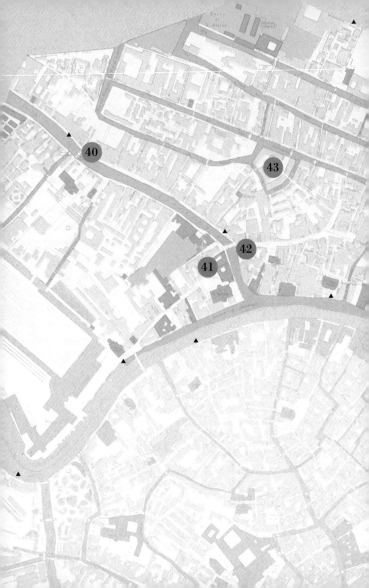

Sestiere di Canneregio

40. Ponte di San Giobbe, also known as dei Tre Archi

The current Ponte di San Giobbe was built by the architect Andrea Tirali in 1688, and replaced a preceding wooden bridge built in 1503, which in its turn had replaced a wooden bridge with three arches which can be seen in Jacopo de' Barbari's map. Tirali's bridge originally had no parapet and had very large, sloping steps. The bridge was probably given its current form in 1794, when the large, sloping steps were changed into groups of smaller steps and when the parapet was added. The parapet may well have added to the security, but unfortunately it has also compromised the elegance of the original construction.

The bridges of Venice were normally single-arch constructions. The only three-arch stone bridge in the 16th century was Ponte San Lorenzo; there were others, of course, but they were wooden, and were mainly drawbridges for ships and other vessels. Apart from San Giobbe, other such bridges were Ponte delle Guglie, Ponte Longo (Giudecca), Ponte di San Pietro and, obviously, Rialto.

Not very far from the bridge, along Fondamenta di Cannaregio and towards the lagoon, there is the unfinished church of Santa Maria dei Penitenti, with an annexed hospice for "redeemed women of questionable morals". In the opposite direction there is Giuseppe Sardi's grandiose 17th century Palazzo Surian-Bellotto, which was leased out to the French Embassy in the 18th century. The philosopher Jean-Jacques Rousseau also lived here for a short while when he was the Ambassador's private secretary. About Venice he wrote that he was particularly "admired of the courtesans, one of whom gave [me] the inestimably important advice to put women aside and study mathematics, and an equally immutable aversion to the government of the Republic".

While the façade is intact, the interior has been profoundly changed (floors were added by halving the height of the original rooms, and the larger halls were divided up into small apartments), and there is nothing left of the original distribution of rooms. The area originally containing a garden, renowned for its size and beauty, now contains a series of nondescript buildings. On the fall of the Republic, the building was turned into the city's Lost Property Office, and is now a large condominium.

The city's abattoirs were on the other side of the canal, along Fondamenta di San Giobbe, beyond Ponte della Saponella. The area was then chosen for a new hospital, projected by Le Corbusier, but "all the clamour surrounding the project eventually boiled down to an abstract notice reading 'Hospital Area'". The notice itself has now disappeared, and the area is currently being used by the University of Venice.

41. Campo San Geremia

Campo San Geremia is currently a sort of through-way, and its urban characteristics are no different now to what they were originally (even though the buildings surrounding the *campo* have been radically modified). The *campo*'s church, founded in the 11th century and rebuilt in the second half of the 13th, was completely overhauled in 1753. The architect Carlo Corbellini gave the new church a Greek cross form, and had its main axis rotated by 90 degrees. Due to funding problems, work was not completed until 1871, when the two façades on Rio di Cannaregio and the Grand Canal were added. The building to the right of the façade is actually a reconstruction of the main headquarters of the Beata Vergine del Suffragio dei Morti (The Holy Virgin for the Relief of the Dead) confraternity, popularly called the Santa Veneranda. It was bombed and destroyed in 1849 during the Austrian siege of the city. The *campanile* is 13th century Romanesque, with the upper sections added during the Gothic period.

Palazzo Labia towers perpendicularly to the left of the church façade giving onto the *campo*. The Labia family, originally from Catalonia, arrived in Venice in the early 16th century and bought Venetian citizenship in 1548 and their noble title in 1646 (for the incredible sum of 300,000 ducats). In the 1680s and 1690s, they had the *palazzo* built, and insisted on a form and style that would reflect the family's grandeur and social status. In fact, the area available to them, their lack of any funding problems and the fact that the building would look out onto the Grand Canal meant that the building could be given appropriate architectural and urban emphasis. The building was further enhanced by Tiepolo's interior decorations, while his collaborator, Gerolamo Mengozzi Colonna, painted incredible architectural tromp-l'oeuils. The project, which was basically baroque and Longhena-like, was by Alessandro Tremignon, later replaced by Cominelli. The most important façade, facing Rio

Cannaregio, is developed according to two orders with enormous round arch windows along a continuous balcony, with impressive column lesenes. The bottom section has an ashlar finish, while the topmost storey is characterised by ogival openings alternated by the family's symbolic eagles. In 18th century Venice the *palazzo* was used for lavish parties and opulent feasts, which culminated in the guests' throwing the silverware and solid gold crockery into the Grand Canal, accompanied by the chant of *"l'abia o non l'abia, sarò sempre Labia"* ("whether I've got it or not, I'll always be a Labia"). Fully aware of the expense involved, however, special nets were placed in the Grand Canal so that the cutlery and crockery could be secretly rescued.

The Labia family lost the building in the early 19th century, and it slowly deteriorated as it went from owner to owner. It was eventually transformed into a series of apartments, the rent from which was used to fund different charities. There were 27 families living in the building in 1940, and the old ballroom was used as a laundry. Soon after it was bought by a private owner, who restored it to its former glory and filled the *palazzo* with antique furniture. In 1951, just before the *palazzo* and its furniture were auctioned off, the owner gave one last masked ball to re-evoke the splendours of 18th century Venice.

The rest of the *campo*, from the Santa Veneranda confraternity to the side of Palazzo Labia, is surrounded by ordinary houses. The *campo* is also well-known for the sporting events that used to be held there. Especially in the 17th century, it was used as an enormous open-air gymnasium, and football matches and bull-fights were held there. One of the most famous took place in the second half of the 18th century, with the Spanish ambassador in attendance, and at the end of which a young Venetian nobleman named Savorgnan actually managed to cut the head off two Hungarian bulls without first having removed their horns.

42. Ponte di Cannaregio, also known as delle Guglie

The current stone bridge was originally built in 1580, and replaced the former three-arched wooden drawbridge (built in 1285 under Doge Dandolo). An inscription on the pilaster on the Cannaregio side of the bridge is dated 1580, and states: "MARCUS BRIZIENSIS – INGENIARIS OFII PROVISORI – COMUNIS". The parish priest Salvadori asked Contini to build the new bridge. It was restored in 1641, in 1777 and just recently, when special steps were added for the physically disabled. It takes its name from the canal, which is the largest and most important of those linking the Grand Canal with the lagoon. Its alternative name, "delle Guglie" or "of the Spires", derives from the four obelisks placed at the ends of the railing.

The first arched stone or marble bridges in Venice had large, sloping steps, almost ramps, used by horses and other four-footed animals, and often had no parapet. Ponte delle Guglie was originally built with these sloping steps but, unlike other bridges of the period, it was given a parapet. There are only two bridges in Venice now that have no parapets: Ponte Chiodo, a private bridge on Rio di San Felice; and Ponte del Diavolo on Torcello. Both of these are very small bridges.

43. Campo del Ghetto Novo – The Ghetto

Campo del Ghetto Novo was the first of the three areas that make up the entire Venetian Ghetto to have been set up as the enforced living quarters for Italian and German Jews (in 1516). It occupies an entire island and is completely surrounded by very tall houses, called "Tower-Houses" in Venetian due to their height (which was dictated by the need to fit as many people as possible into the Ghetto). Only two bridges led to the *campo*, and both had large doors that could be locked from the outside. One was on Fondamenta degli Ormesini; the other linked Ghetto Novo with Ghetto Vecchio. A third area was added in 1633, and was called Ghetto Nuovissimo. It is believed that this is when the third bridge was added, as it would have linked the three ghettos. The bridge, in fact, is called Ponte del Ghetto Nuovissimo.

In the 11th-13th centuries there was apparently a very large Jewish community in Venice, probably on the Giudecca. In 1349, it was decreed that Jews could not stay in Venice for any longer than a fortnight, and that they had to wear a piece of yellow cloth on their breast. The yellow cloth eventually gave way to a yellow circle which had to be worn on the subject's cloak, and then, in the early 16th century, a red hat. In 1509, masses of German and Italian Jewish refugees began to arrive and settle in Venice, and relations with the local inhabitants were not idyllic. This led to a decree dated March 29th 1516, in which the Serenissima stated that "all Jews are to live united in Corte de Case, which is in the Ghetto in the vicinity of San Girolamo; in order that they not go about at night a large door shall be placed on either bridge leading to the Ghetto, which door shall be opened in the morning at dawn and locked at midnight by four Gentile custodians who shall be paid by the Jews themselves. Moneys to be paid these custodians shall be established by the current Council…"

The area indicated in the decree is the current Ghetto Nuovo, so named to distinguish it from Ghetto Vecchio, which extended from the current

campo to Rio Cannaregio. The whole area was used for smelting metals (called *"getti"*), and eventually provided the term by which any area used for the segregation of ethnic groups became known.

Besides curfews and enforced dress-codes, Jews were also subjected to an extremely rigid discipline which virtually forbade them any form of carnal intercourse with non-Jewish women, even prostitutes. They were also debarred from any of the noble arts, except for medicine; they were equally debarred from any manual art or craft. They were also forbidden to buy houses or any other property.

The various ethnic or national groups maintained their customs, and built separate synagogues (but only according to Serenissima law, which allowed synagogues provided they could not be identified as such from the outside). There are now three synagogues in Campo del Ghetto Nuovo: the Scuola Tedesca (or German Synagogue), the Scuola Italian (or Italian Synagogue) and the Scuola del Canton. According to some, the name for this latter derives from the Venetian word for "corner" (i.e. *"canton"* – the synagogue is built on just such a corner); according to others, the name derives from the Cantoni family, who gave funds for its construction.

Ghetto Nuovo is much the same now as it was centuries ago, except for the shops that must have been present originally (currently there are only a few little shops for tourists) and for the northern area, which was demolished in the 19th century to make way for an old people's home.

Compared to the traditional Venetian *campo*, Ghetto Nuovo has no imposing building façade giving onto it, nor is there any religious building acting as the focal point for the *campo* or opening onto a canal or *rio*. The *campo*'s fascination derives from its ring of disparate houses, which, taken together, constitute an original and quirky skyline.

44. Campo dei Mori and Casa di Tintoretto

Just after Ponte dei Mori, on the corner of Campo dei Mori, you will come across a stone figure wearing oriental clothes. The *campo* has a triangular shape towards Calle dei Mori, and eventually leads to Ponte della Madonna dell'Orto. On the wall to your right there are a further two figures – and a fourth figure can be found on the *fondamenta*. Tradition has it that these four Moorish figures represent the three Mastelli brothers, Greek merchants who arrived from Morea in 1112, and who were therefore known as Moors. The fourth figure, however, simply represents a merchant. The names of the four figures are (as you see them coming from the corner and moving towards the *calle*) Mori, Rioba, Sandi and Afani. They date from the 13th century, and have been placed on fragments from Roman altars.

The right of the *campo* contains a complex of buildings that go from Rio della Sensa (Ascension) to Rio della Madonna dell'Orto. This complex was built by the Mastelli family, and one of the buildings (which contemporary chronicles defined as "very honourable") is Palazzo Cammello, so called because of the bas-relief of a camel on the façade giving onto Rio della Madonna dell'Orto. This *palazzo* is the only one that is still in good condition, while the others in the *campo* with the statues were rebuilt in 1918 after they had been bombed. On the other side of the campo there are buildings with Gothic and Renaissance elements.

In 1202, the Mastelli family participated in the Crusade led by Doge Enrico Dandolo. After the Crusade, the family opened a warehouse for spices, and again used the camel as an insignia. The family later moved its concerns and headquarters to the mainland, where the last family member, named Antonio, died in 1620. Out of deference to this last member of the family, the fourth of the figures mentioned above is also referred to as Antonio. This figure, along with that of the Hunchback of Rialto (which can be seen holding up the stairs in Campo Rialto), were used

for the Venetian mask known as Il Pasquino dei Veneziani, and which was used by authors of satires.

The fourth figure can be seen on the outer wall of the *palazzo* belonging to the Robusti family, just off Fondamenta dei Mori on Rio della Sensa. This building probably also belonged to the same unit of buildings built by the Mastelli family. This is a 15th century Gothic house, with triforate windows, and where the windows along the *piano nobile* framed by cornices with cord-like decorations. Tintoretto, who painted the cycle in Scuola di San Rocco and the famous works in Madonna dell'Orto and the Doge's Palace, was born in this house in 1518, and died here on May 31st, 1594. His father Battista was a fabric dyer, and it was from the Venetian word for "dyer", *tintor*, that Tintoretto's name derived.

45. Abbey and Church of the Misericordia

The complex that is now known as the Misericordia is actually made up of three buildings: the church, the abbey and the Scuola Nuova. The church was founded in 936, and two further institutions were "superimposed" on the church – the religious institution of the Monastery of Santa Maria di Valverde and that of the confraternity or Scuola of the Misericordia. The church itself belonged to the convent, and in the 12th century it was transformed from Byzantine to Gothic, and its exterior was renovated in 1649 by the Bolognese architect Clemente Moli, one of Bernini's followers. On the façade over the main doorway, Moli placed a bust of Senator Gaspare Moro, to whose family jurisdictional power over the convent had been devolved during the 1348 plague. The church's interior was repeatedly altered, especially during the 19th century. The *campanile*, on the contrary, has remained structurally unchanged. The Misericordia confraternity is mentioned in official documents for the first time in 1261, while the Scuola itself was constituted in 1308. Originally, there was a statue over the main doorway (now in the entrance to the nearby Corte Nova), which was replaced by a sculpture of Bartolomeo Bon (in its turn removed, and now in the Victoria and Albert Museum, London). It was decided in the 16th century to build the Scuola Nuova and a building in Corte Nova (the Scuola Nuova was originally intended to be a hospice for the Abbey). Work began in 1508 (the original project was by Alessandro Leopardi under Tullio Lombardi's direction; the project was abandoned and replaced by another by Jacopo Sansovino), and completed in 1589.

The confraternity was disbanded by Napoleonic decree on November 26th, 1806. The building later became a sports centre, and the upper floor was turned into a basketball court. The Scuola Vecchia became a studio for the painter Italico Brass. It currently houses an art collection and is used for university activities.

46. Ponte Molin de la Racheta

The *insula* between Rio San Felice and Rio de la Racheta was one of the first to be settled in Venice, and was almost certainly reclaimed and built up before the 13th century. The *insula* follows an urban plan which is typical of rectangular areas (see chapter 28). The longitudinal *calle* which links the whole built-up area is called Calle de la Racheta ("of the Racquet"), and is joined to the other islands via Ponte Molin de la Racheta and Ponte Priuli. Ponte Molin takes its name from the erudite scholar Antonio Molin, who, in the 18th century, lived in the small 15th century Gothic building that gives onto Canale Santa Caterina and Canale di Noale (it can be reached through Sottoportico Molin a the foot of the bridge in Calle Racheta). Sottoportico Molin leads to Rio Noale, and affords a wonderful view of the Misericordia complex (see chapter 45). On the other side of the *calle*, the bridge flanks a walled garden, the foundations of the Gothic Palazzo Molin which was demolished in 1819 (all that is left of this building is the wall with a decorated corner pilaster). The name "Racheta" (i.e. "Racquet") comes from the name Venetians gave to the game "*Jeux de Paume*" or "*Tenez*" (which, through various corruptions, led to the word "*tennis*" in English) and handball (which had been played in Italy since the Middle Ages). The game was originally played with the bare hand, but eventually the racquet was introduced, thus leading to the name "Racquet Ball". Racquet ball courts were built in the San Cassiano and Biri area, as well as along the "long road between Santa Caterina and San Felice", which was later called Calle de la Racheta. On the other side of the bridge there is the Gothic church of Santa Caterina, with its monastery and cloister. Napoleon suppressed the religious complex in 1807 and founded a boarding school called Foscarini, for which the church was originally used as an oratory and later as a gymnasium. The boarding school is still in use, while the church is currently inaccessible to the general public.

47. Church of the Gesuiti

The original convent was founded in the mid-12th century by the Cruciferous Order, and was rebuilt following a disastrous fire in 1214. The rebuilding also entailed a new church, a cloister, a hospice and a hospital along the current bank of Rio dei Gesuiti. In that period, and up to the late 16th century, the lagoon extended to the current Fondamenta Nuove. The house of Titian – from whose garden on a clear day you could see the Cadore mountains – was in fact on the banks of the lagoon, while now it is well ensconced in Calle dei Botteri. In 1514, after another fire, the complex was partly reconstructed with its current form. Both the Senate and the Holy See threatened on several occasions to confiscate the order's goods, to expel them from Venice and to disband them because of their licentious and immoral behaviour. They were finally suppressed by Pope Alexander VI in 1650, and all their possessions were confiscated by the Serenissima, who then auctioned them off in 1657. They were bought for 50,000 ducats by the Jesuits, who had themselves been expelled from Venice in 1606 because of their stand in the affair that pitted the Serenissima against Pope Paul V. It is said that on that occasion, as their superior was blessing the crowds, the large boat carrying the Jesuits lost its moorings; the Jesuits themselves were then greeted by jeers from the crowds. The Jesuits eventually rebuilt the church in its current form, according to a project by Domenico Rossi, and it was completed in 1750. The building is characterised by its Latin cross form with single nave; its façade is imbued with a sense of dynamism thanks to the interaction between its different planes and the numerous statues lining the cornice along the first storey and tympanum, with its refined and abundant decorations. The interior is just as dynamic. The church is, for Venice, a singular cultural as well as religious artefact, and is well worth the visit.

48. Ponte Donà and Palazzo Donà

Fondamenta Nuove were built in early 1589 under Doge Pasquale Cicogna, and were supposed to go from Santa Giustina right up to Sant'Alvise; they eventually went no further than Sacca della Misericordia. Ponte Donà, built in 1842, is very wide and spans one of the largest *rii* in Venice; its arch is very open and polycentric, and is decorated with Istrian stone. The bridge, however, appears to have two quite different "characters": if viewed from the canal, where only the middle section stretching from the Convento dei Gesuiti to Palazzo Donà can be seen, it seems to assume the essential character and sobriety of colour of a triumphal arch; if viewed from the lagoon, however, from where you can see it continuing along Fondamenta Nuove, its form is much ampler and its profile a much more relaxed polygonal shape.

At the foot of the bridge there is Palazzo Donà delle Rose. This is one of the very few *palazzi* in Venice still owned and inhabited by the founding family, and it still has the original décor and works of art created for the various rooms, as well as a well-kept family archive. The building was begun by Doge Leonardo Donà on March 24th 1610. Originally, the site was most definitely on the outskirts of Venice and very sparsely inhabited. The project was probably an elaboration of a design by the Doge's friend, Paolo Sarpi. The building is perfectly in keeping both with the character of the Doge himself and his careful and responsible handling of the public funds that probably went into the building – in fact the building seems to be a reaction against the dominant Classical tastes of the time, and seems to hark back to the austerity of a by-gone Venice, an austerity which was seen to be one of the fundamental reasons for the Serenissima's greatness. Leonardo's brother, Nicolò, was apparently incensed at the stylistic choices made, and it is said that a fight between the two brothers over the issue led to Leonardo's death in 1612.

49. Church of Santa Maria dei Miracoli

The Miracoli church was built between 1481 and 1489 by the architect Pietro Lombardo. It is one of the most stylistically "compact" Renaissance churches in Venice. It is such a compact building, and so perfectly suited to its surroundings, that you almost get the impression that it was originally built elsewhere and then transported and mounted in its current spot almost as if it were a jewel. The church has a single nave with a decorated wooden box ceiling. Above the entrance, the choir area was linked to the nearby monastery via an overhead walkway (destroyed in 1865). The presbytery occupies the entire apse area, and is much higher than the rest of the church's floor; it can be reached by a large set of steps. The wealth of decorations, the multi-coloured marbles and the bas-reliefs made by deft *tajapiera* (or "stonecutters") under Lombardo's close scrutiny make the church the most precious of buildings, a special container for the only relic it contains – an image of Santa Maria dei Miracoli (Our Lady of Miracles). According to tradition, in fact, the church was built in honour of the image of the Madonna which was once placed on the corner of a house in Corte Nova and which was considered miraculous. To keep the vast crowds who flocked to see the image under control, the Amadi family temporarily housed the painting in a wooden chapel which they had built in their private courtyard. Using money donated by the faithful and the Amadi family itself, the current church was eventually built. The architect Lombardo was called in on January 25th 1481, when work began. The church was completed in 1489. The church was built so quickly that Lombardo could supervise the entire process, thus making the coherence in style and execution possible. Another of the church's important aspects is that it is one of the very few in Venice that has not been subsequently rebuilt or restructured.

50. Corte Morosini

Half-way along the right-hand side of the church of San Giovanni Crisostomo there is Calle del Cagnoletto. Along this *calle*, to the right, there is a *sottoportico* which leads to Corte Amadi, and a second *sottoportico* leading to Corte Morosini. The entrance itself is dark and gloomy, and above the Istrian stone architrave there is a 13th-14th century marble arch. Two checked frames surround a *fascia* which is sculpted with geometric designs. The marble slab surmounted by the arch contains a coat-of-arms in bas-relief and a crest. Above the arch there is a round patera containing two little birds. Two further bits of marble over the arch and patera have, yes, protected the structure from rain, but have led to its corrosion. Corte Morosini opens up just round the corner. The court is Gothic, paved with terracotta tiles and contains a well-head in the Veneto-Byzantine style and two uncovered staircases. It was from this court (and in part from Corte Amadi) that visitors gained access to the surrounding buildings which, in the 11th century, constituted a complex belonging to the Morosini family. The main building is the 15th century Ca' Morosini, which juts out onto Rio del Fontego dei Tedeschi, and which is on the corner of Rio dei Miracoli. Particularly interesting is the façade of the Gothic Ca' Amadi, with its squared triforate windows and small central balcony with two pink marble lions on either corner, which can be seen from Ponte de l'Ogio. Corte Morosini is one of the most difficult to find of the numerous courts in this area, and is well outside of any of the well-beaten tourist routes. Most probably it was originally intended as the central courtyard for the series of houses which, along with those of the Polo family in Corte del Milion, were considered the Morosini family's own "fortified palace" in the 9th and 10th centuries.

51. Church of San Giovanni Grisostomo

The church of San Giovanni Crisostomo, rebuilt in its current Renaissance style between 1497 and 1504, was the architect Mauro Codussi's last work. His son Domenico completed the church, and supervised the two doorways and the windows on the façade. The church, which was built in an area with the greatest concentration of buildings in Venice, is tightly tucked in between two flanking buildings. The façade gives onto a *calle*, and the apse is hemmed in by houses. It is only along its two sides that there is some form of "breathing space", with a small *campo* providing a bit of breathing space. The *campanile* was built in 1531-32, and has since never been modified.

The first church on the site was built in the 11th century, when there was most likely much more space, with its *campanile* slightly to one side in front of the façade. In the same period, the houses steadily began to be built around the church, isolating the church itself. At the end of the 15th century, the church was in such poor shape (due to a fire in the nearby Polo family houses) that it was completely demolished (1495) and rebuilt. Even though Pope Innocent VIII himself tried to raise funds for the church's reconstruction (he even conceded special indulgences for donors), the amount of money raised was insufficient and Codussi was therefore not able to add ornamental decorations. However, the "essentialist" style of the church and the lack of marble decorations (simple coloured plasters were used instead) have actually underlined the fascinating geometry of the church's lines and volumes. The subsequent decision to move the *campanile* so as to align it with the façade came from the Senate, who also decided to have some of the houses in front of the church demolished, thus providing a bit of relief for the otherwise congested Renaissance church. The harmony of the church's proportions was compromised when the *calle* in front of the church was raised, thus covering the socle and steps leading to the doorway.

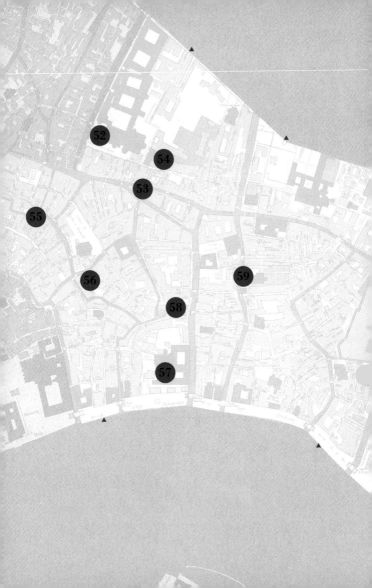

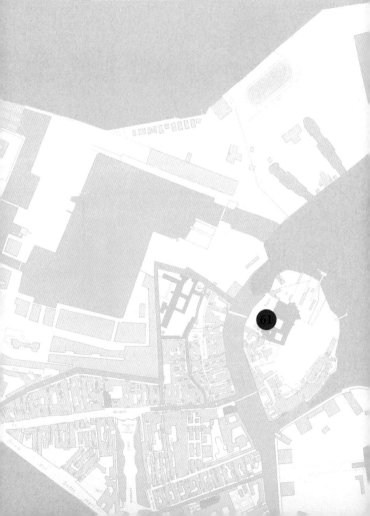

52. Campo Santi Giovanni e Paolo

After St Mark's square, this *campo* is the city's most important in terms of monuments, size and the amazing quality of its urban space. It lies mid-way between the older centres of the city – namely St Mark's, Rialto and the Arsenale (i.e., those areas that denote power, commerce and occupation). The area evolved progressively between the 13th and 17th centuries, both in measured and balanced terms, but also with a great sense of invention and force, from the initial construction of the church and convent, to the *scuola*, the equestrian monument and the *palazzi* themselves. The best vantage point, from which you can best appreciate the *campo*'s perspective views offered by the water and land, is along Calle del Forno on the Rio dei Mendicanti, between Ponte Rosso and Ponte Cavallo. >From here you will have a perfect view of that exhilarating space defined by the grandiose façade of the Basilica di Santi Giovanni e Paolo, and which is firmly centred in the marvellous equestrian monument dedicated to Bartolomeo Colleoni.

Legend has it that in 1234, following a dream, Doge Jacopo Tiepolo donated to the Dominican order the swampy land surrounding a modest oratory dedicated to St Daniel in the area now occupied by the church. The lagoon, at that stage, began just behind the Scuola. Much land was later reclaimed, and thanks to funds bequeathed by patrons and donations from the Serenissima the church was finally built. It was consecrated in 1430, when building on the convent began on the reclaimed land (which eventually included enough land for two cloisters and a courtyard). The convent was completely restructured according to Baroque canons in 1630, following a project by Longhena. The Basilica, dedicated to Saints John and Paul ("Giovanni" and "Paolo" in Italian, blending in Venetian to form "Zanipolo"), was from the very outset chosen by the Doges for their burial. After the 15th century, the Senate decreed that all Doges' funerals were to be held there. The Basilica has three naves, with 15th century stained glass windows on the right-hand side of the transept and also originally had a large central wooden choir (dismantled in 1682) similar to the choir stalls in the Frari. On the left-hand side of the transept there is the Madonna del Rosario chapel, built in 1575 in order to give thanks for the victorious Battle of Lepanto. The chapel was rebuilt after the 1867 fire.

The Scuola di San Marco, one of the six large *scuole* of the city, was set up in San Zanipolo in 1437 when the Dominicans conceded the area surrounding the church. In 1485, only five years after completion, the original building was destroyed by fire. Lombardo, Buora and di Dominico worked together on the new Renaissance building. Codussi and Sansovino later finished the work. The façade is divided into two distinct parts (the "temple" on the left, the "hospice" on the right), and is characterised by both the beauty and lightness of the decorations and trompe-l'oeuil perspectives on the four panels surrounding the doorways, as well as the rhythm of the crowning apparatus, which derives from the series of semicircular frontons topped by statues and other decorative elements. The equestrian monument has its own singular history. When Colleoni, a mercenary commander of the Venetian army, died in 1475, he left the Republic 100,000 Ducats on the proviso that a monument be dedicated to him "in front of St Mark's". Even though the Serenissima had never allowed any monument to be built anywhere in the city, let alone in St Mark's Square, it nonetheless granted Colleoni his wish – albeit with a slight twist. St Mark's it would be, but not St Mark's Square – the Scuola San Marco would have to do. The work was designed and realised mainly by Verrocchio, who died before completion. Despite the artist's own wishes, the Serenissima called in Alessandro Leonardi who, in the courtyard now known as "Del Cavallo" ("of the horse") near Madonna dell'Orto, finally put the statue together and added his own base.

The *campo* is closed off on three sides by houses and *palazzi*, the more important of which are the 18th century Palazzo Dandolo (with its typical truncated-cone drum chimneys) and Palazzo Morosini (with two triforate windows with columns). The *campo* was covered in grass until 1835, as can be evinced from the strips of Istrian stone.

Currently, the convent and *scuola*, as well as the Mendicanti hospice built along the Rio Dei Mendicanti, house the city's hospital complex.

53. Corte Bottera al Ponte dei Conzafelci

The Bridge of the Conzafelci (who looked after the gondola booths) crosses the Rio del Pestrin where it breaks off to form the two rios of San Giovanni Laterano I and II. The *insula* of San Giovanni Laterano has an elongated triangular shape reminiscent of a ship whose prow separates the two rios. The outline is constituted by the 17th century Palazzetto Tetta, named after the original owners, who arrived from Sebenico in 1611. Along the wider section of the *insula*, to the left, there is a bank with a round arch which constitutes the entrance along the canal to Corte Bottera. The current walkway entrance is a marble gallery which leads to the ramp of a bridge and then a *sottoportico* with a set of descending steps. Corte Bottera is off the beaten track, and the entrance is so hidden that not even all Venetians are aware of it. It has a characteristic "primitive" plan and archaic constructive elements, some of which are presumably remains taken from the home of the Contarini dalla Zogia family when it was demolished. The gothic columns that hold up the large wooden architrave of the *sottoportico*, the late-Gothic well-head, the 14th century staircase with stone steps, the beautiful 13th century arch illustrated with animal and leaf motifs (incredibly, the arch was split up in the 19th century to make way for a window). It is difficult to isolate the lines of the 15th century construction, however there appear to be the fundamental elements of a *fondaco* house, i.e. two entrances (one from the canal, the other from the Corte via a portal-arch leading to Barbaria delle Tole), the external staircase leading to the *piano nobile* (indicated by the Serliana), a second internal staircase and the storage rooms. The current state of the complex, the end result of the demands made on the area over the centuries, is not of the best, and it really should be set right. But Corte Bottera, despite this, has retained the flavour of the "real" Venice, which has somehow managed to escape the impositions of "modernisation", thus giving the visitor a rare glimpse of the feelings and rhythms of a different era.

54. Ospedaletto

In 1527-1528, the Serenissima founded a hospice for the old and infirm in Barbaria delle Tole. The original building was called the "Bersaglio" (or "target") because of the military activities it housed. The church of Santa Maria dei Derelitti was annexed to the hospice, and therefore officially became the Ospedaletto church. *Forestiere illuminato* (1740) had the following to say about Ospedaletto: "The Hospital is annexed to the Church. This Hospital takes in the ill until they are recovered, all pilgrims for three days, and a certain number of little orphans; all until such a time as the males may be employed in some profession that will allow them to provide for themselves, and the females fixed in matrimony or placed in monasteries consecrated to Our Lord". Work on the Hospice was finally completed in 1662 based on projects by Giuseppe Sardi, who was later replaced by Baldassarre Longhena. Longhena not only completed Sardi's work, but also completely renovated the church and redid the façade. Though it is true that the benefactor Cargnoni wanted a work that would "make people forget the name of "Ospedaletto", or "hospital", but that could, with reason, be called a Hospice", the richness, plasticity, *chiaroscuro*, the forward jutting of the building and the courage displayed in some of the works are nonetheless overwhelming. Now, after having been cleaned, the massive white vortex of pilasters, enormous masks and statues is an imposing sight for the overwhelmed visitors, who nonetheless might find themselves amused and even moved by façade. It must be said that the young orphan girls were introduced to music, much as they were at the Zitelle. For 200 years, teaching took place in the church's little choir, near the organ just above the main altar. In the 18th century, Matteo Lucchesi added a music room to the hospice. The room, which is a must for visitors, is still exactly as it was, and includes frescoes by Jacopo Guarana and Agostino Mengozzi Colonna.

55. Calle del Paradiso

Calle del Paradiso is situated between Ponte del Paradiso on the Santa Maria Formosa canal and Salizada di San Lio. It is characterised by an uninterrupted flow of *barbacani* along both sides and by two arches over the Calle at the two extremities. Building took place from the 12th to the 16th centuries. Calle del Paradiso is the only example of a *calle* entirely lined with *barbacani*, which are so typically Venetian, and where private and public buildings are intermingled. *Barbacani* are nothing other than wooden boards and beams that were used to support the jutting upper floors of buildings (sometimes these storeys jut up to a meter beyond the ground floor!). This guaranteed greater living space for the upper storeys, while the shops along the ground floor were provided with a protective overhang and the *calle* itself was larger than it would otherwise have been. Generally, however, *barbacani* were limited to only one side of the *calle*: here the novelty is that they are used on both sides. The elegance of the two Gothic arches at the two ends of the *calle* contrasts with the sobriety of the two long walls.

The arch giving onto Ponte del Paradiso is, in fact, a rich marble pinnacle, with the Foscari coat-of-arms on the one side and the Foscari-Mocenigo coat-of-arms on the other, added to celebrate the marriage of Pellegrina Foscari and Alvise Mocenigo dalle Zogie in 1491. The second is a real, much more straightforward arch.

The most interesting construction, albeit its mixed 12-16th century styles, is the *palazzetto* on Rio Santa Maria Formosa, which is to the left as you go over the bridge from the *calle*. Almost all the buildings in the *calle* belonged to the Pomposa abbey, as can be deduced from the inscription on a plaque to the left of the arch giving onto Salizada San Lio. The name of the *calle* and bridge derives from the exceptional *luminarie*, or lights and candles, made for feast days and especially for Good Friday.

56. Campiello Querini Stampalia

Campiello Querini Stampalia is characterised by a bizarre "static" quality, is devoid of unnecessary ornament and additions, and is closed off on three sides by smooth façades giving straight onto the canal or the *campiello*. It is only towards Santa Maria Formosa that the volumes of the buildings become more varied as they give onto the church itself. There are two smaller houses facing the *campiello*: a modest yellow one, and a more rigidly-structured green house with more pretentious 19th century decorations. Just behind them you can see the massive forms of the Scuola dei Bombardieri, built in 1598 by the Bombardieri confraternity (who had their own altar in the church of San Barnaba, with a famous painting of the saint by Palma the Elder). Originally, Ponte Pasqualigo Avogadro led to two corner *palazzi*: the Baroque Palazzo Avogadro and the Gothic Palazzo Venier (which now has its own private bridge from the *campiello*). Palazzo Querini Stampalia, which gives the name to the *campiello*, is right next to Palazzo Avogadro and flanks the long *rio* and curves away to fit in with the *caranto*. A *caranto* is a form of land which was used for the deeper, underlying foundations of a building, and which was totally exploited by Venetian builders, even if it meant introducing curving façades. The Querini Stampalia family, a branch of the Querini family, had the *palazzo* built in 1528, and kept it until 1868, when the family died out. A foundation bearing the family name was then set up which donated the *palazzo*'s artistic and library heritage to the city, and made its study rooms and museums available to the general public (in fact, opening hours are alternative to those of other institutions in the city). The name "Stampalia" was originally a nick-name, corrupted from the Aegean island of Astypalia, which was owned by the family and to which the family fled in 1310 after having been exiled for taking part in the Bajamonte Tiepolo plot. There is now a small bridge in wood and iron, by the architect Carlo Scarpa, which leads to the building from the *campiello*.

57. Campo della Bragora

The name "Bragora" comes from the name given to one of the two very similar and adjacent *insulae* in Castello (because they were so close and so similar they were known as "The Twins"). The term probably ultimately derives from the muddy, swampy area the *campo* was originally built in (from "*bra-go*", mud and/or silt, and "*gora*", stagnant water). Others maintain that the etymology is "*bragolare*", or from "*bragole*", the name given to local merchants, from the Greek "*agorà*" ("to argue", "to engage in battle"), or even from the twins Castor and Pollux and the eastern "*b'ragal*" ("two men"). Campo della Bragora is a closed *campo*, large enough not to feel too hemmed in by the surrounding buildings. The most imposing building is Palazzo Gritti Badoer, a 14th century Gothic construction with a large five-light window surrounded by a check frame with marble decorations. The balustrade dates from the 16th century. The façade is covered in *altinelle*, i.e. small terracotta bricks; although originally frescoed, it is now in a very poor state. The adjacent Palazzo Soderini was the house of Attilio and Emilio Bandiera, two brothers who lost their life, along with Domenico Moro, fighting for the liberation of Italy in 1844. The *campo* is therefore also known as Campo Bandiera e Moro. Between the two buildings there is a dead-end *calle* called Calle della Morte (i.e. "of Death"), apparently because prisoners condemned to death by the Council of Ten were once executed there.

There are no other particularly interesting elements or buildings surrounding the *campo* except for the church of San Giovanni Battista and the adjacent 17th century building, which is relegated to a corner of the *campo* and flanked by buildings which do nothing to confer interest or highlight it. The church, according to popular tradition, was founded in the 8th century, but there are no official documents until 1090. The current Gothic aspect dates from the 1475 reconstruction. Subsequent work modified the decorative elements, and particularly the central choir area, the original of which is now almost entirely lost. The original *campanile*, which according to Jacopo de' Barbari's plans had a pinnacle and Gothic niches, was demolished and replaced with a small structure. The façade is exquisitely simple, without any accentuation of the partitions through the use of marble, sculptures or niches. The crowning over the doorway , the rosette and the upper areas of the building are the epitome of sobriety. However, the building wing, which is elegant and well-balanced and in which the church is totally immersed, unfortunately complicates the dominant simplicity of the church, and seems to bear no rational relationship with the church itself. To the left of the façade, a meter or so behind it, are the main offices of the ex-Scuola di San Giovanni Battista and that of the Santissimo Sacramento (i.e. "The Holy Sacrament", as can be evinced from the two marble chalices above the ground floor windows), which joined the former in 1581.

One of the most famous members of the congregation was the so-called "red priest" Antonio Vivaldi, who was born to one of the Marciana chapel's violinists in 1678 and baptised in the church on May 6th, 1678. He was ordained in 1703, but was soon dispensed from religious office due to poor health. In the same year he became a violin teacher at Ospedale della Pietà, one of the hospices for orphans and children of the very poor, where the children were taught music. Ospedale della Pietà is very close to the church and even closer to Calle del Dose, where Vivaldi originally lived (he later moved to the house on the corner between Campo Santi Filippo e Giacomo and Calle Rimpeto la Sacrestia). Ospedale della Pietà became the centre of all his activities, as can be seen from the Ospedale's official documents over the years. Even when he had to leave Venice to tour Europe (the musical scene at that time in Venice was extremely productive, and was very closely linked to the rest of Europe), the Ospedale would allow him to "leave this city for one month, for the deployment of his virtuous applications; the pious congregation may rest assured that on his return he will dedicate himself with fervour and spirit to his normal tasks". Vivaldi died in Vienna in c. 1741.

58. Scuola di San Giorgio degli Schiavoni

The Scuola di San Giorgio degli Schiavoni was founded on March 24, 1451. Under the protection of Saints George, Jerome and Tryphone, its aim was to welcome Dalmatians, mainly sailors and craftsmen, who had moved to Venice in large numbers in the 15th century. The original *scuola* was housed in the nearby church of San Giovanni al Tempio, which belonged to the Templars (now the Knights of Malta). At the beginning of the 16th century, the Dalmatians raised funds to build the *scuola* on its current site. In 1551 the *scuola*'s exterior was renovated, and sculptures and marble statues were added. There are two halls inside - the one upstairs was used for meetings, and contains a small room known as the *albergo* (i.e. "hotel"); the one downstairs is used for religious services and has a sacristy (containing museum pieces and a *Mariegola*, or book of statutes). Along the walls of the downstairs room you can see the nine paintings by Carpaccio (1502-1508) which make up four hagiographic cycles. The Scuola's artistic heritage is still intact mainly thanks to Prince Eugène Bonaparte, who, in response to a request made by the Scuola's then-head guardian, decreed that "this last bastion of the Schiavoni" was to be protected by all means. The Scuola now offers us a part of Venice's Renaissance heritage, so radically different from the city's monumental solemnity. In the small and welcoming dimensions of an oratory, the Scuola fascinates and leads us to discover an area of Venice in which works of the highest calibre can still be admired in their original context. They therefore interact with us as they would have done when they were originally placed in the Scuola, and are therefore so close to our daily lives.

The area surrounding the Scuola, unfortunately, was not so lucky: the buildings along the *fondamenta* were extended vertically. Ponte della Commenda was added and the entire *riva* facing Rio della Pietà, originally a vast expanse of lawns and grass, was built up towards San Lorenzo.

59. Calle Magno

Eastwards, along the longitudinal axis of Campo Due Pozzi, we have Calle Magno, so-called because of the old Magno houses situated in the *calle*. It is thought that these houses originally belonged to the Dalle Boccole family, which were still in the area in 1483 when a carpenter, Luigi Goffritto, murdered Francesco Dalle Boccole while he was talking with friends in the *calle*. The severity of Venetian justice is attested to by the fact that Goffritto, who had fled the city, was sentenced to perpetual exile from all the dominions of the Serenissima. He was identified and captured in Capo d'Istria three years later, brought back to Venice, and, according to Tassini, "decapitated 'twixt the two columns of the *piazzetta*, after having had his hand cut off *in loco delicti* [at the scene of the crime]". To the right, just beyond the half-way mark of the *calle*, we have the Gothic Palazzo Magno Bembo. It is difficult to fully appreciate the architectural characteristics of the building because the *calle* itself is so narrow, and because all the buildings are so close together and in a precarious state. The building is famous because of its internal courtyard, where a high interlinked colonnade holds up the upper storey with a wooden architrave with an owl's beak, and its beautiful external staircase (14th century), held up by rounded arches and with an astragal motif along the handrail and the bull's-head step heads. Again on the right of the *calle*, just before Palazzo Magno Bembo, there is Calle dell'Angelo. You will have to walk under a very low *sottoportico* with entrance surmounted by a brick arch and a marble semicircle. Within the semicircle you will find an angel in the act of blessing, whose halo and left wing have been ruined. Flanking the angel there are two noble family shields within two chequered frames. Thanks to its exposure to the elements, the angel is now completely white and in much better shape than the shields, which have been blackened and ruined. However, if you look closely you can make out the "curl" that indicates the Rizzo family, who owned some of the buildings in the area.

60. Arsenale

The Arsenale, or dockyards, constituted the main area of employment for the city of Venice. From as early as the 11th century, the city's power was defined by its mercantile and military naval prowess. In that period Venice's economy was in full flourish thanks to trade with the East. At the same time, tension was mounting with the Holy Land, and this would eventually require an increase, in both qualitative and quantitative terms, in Venice's maritime forces. In order to produce and maintain the sea-craft needed for the city's expansionistic policies, the *squeri* (small boat-building yards) throughout the city were no longer deemed viable. The Serenissima therefore decided to build and manage a large public *squero*, eventually known as the Arsenale. For logistic and security reasons, the area chosen for the Arsenale was between La Bragora and the island of Olivolo, situated near Barbaria delle Tole (which is where timber and wood was delivered from the mainland). It was easily enough reached from St Mark's Basin, and at the same time it could easily be protected from possible attacks from the port area. This is therefore where building began (you can in fact still see the original wet-dock for 24 vessels, protected by high walls and chained off from the rest of the city), and is now called the Arsenale Vecchio. "Arsenale" as a term most probably derives from the Arab *dâr as-sinâa*, which means "the house of trade, job or occupation" (interestingly enough, this was the name of one of the buildings of the period). Initially, activity at the Arsenale was mainly limited to maintenance and organisation. However, in 1122 the workers were pushed to give of their best to produce more than 100 galleys for the victorious Battle of Tyre against the Muslims, as they were again in the early 13th century when the Arsenale built about 200 ships for the Fourth Crusade. Expanded activities and the Republic's involvement in wildly expensive naval operations led to the Arsenale's extension during the first three decades of the 14th century. At the same time, sea-travel and work methods were profoundly reorganised. The second Arsenale area, now known as the Arsenale Nuovo, and the wooden building called The Corderie (an enormous shed-like structure used to work hemp) both date from this period. At the same time plans were made to use canons on both civil and military ships. Thanks to these innovations, the Arsenale made incredible strides in the technological and organisational fields, both in terms of quality and importance, and it began to deploy production-line methods – an incredible innovation for the period. In the 15th and 16th centuries the Arsenale was further extended with the addition of the Arsenale Nuovissimo and other structures. The surrounding walls became even more imposing when 18 lookout towers were added. Extensions came to an end by the late 16th century, by which stage the Arsenale was known as the "heart of the Veneto State". It was to remain substantially unchanged until the end of the Republic. To give some idea of the size and enormous potential of the Arsenale, suffice it to say that in the 15th century the Venetian fleet consisted of about 3,300 ships, of which 3,000 were cargo vessels and the remainder galleys, with crews of 17,000 and 8,000 men respectively. 16,000 *marangoni* (i.e. carpenters) were employed there! The need for structures able to provide services and support or collateral goods, as well as the housing and logistical needs of those working at the Arsenale and their families, profoundly conditioned the urban structure of Castello as well as social life in the area. Remnants can still be found in the place-names. Residential areas were set up along the three land sides of the surrounding walls, and the supply structures were also set up in the surrounding area. Of these structures, the *biscotto* (or dry biscuit) works was publicly-owned, and there were 32 facilities. The *biscotto* was the basic foodstuff supplied to crews and garrisons stationed in distant protectorates and dominions. The quality must have been exceptional, considering that a store of *biscotti* found in Candia in 1821, originally produced in 1669, were still edible! The last two hundred years of the Arsenale's life were beset by external problems which the Serenissima no longer had the force or will to address. From within, the Serenissima was slowed down by enormous bureaucratic strain and undermined by a generalised sense of moral degradation (see, for example, the large number of cases of administrative fraud, thefts

and absent bureaucratic officials recorded in the period). It was only in 1684 (the war against the Turks) and 1715-18 (the War of Corfu) that production levels increased, due to the need to produce supplies for the war effort; but once the wars came to an end, production levels dropped again. To this must be added the fact that the Serenissima was by now much more interested in the Italian "mainland".

At the fall of the Republic on May 12 1797, the Arsenale was still completely intact, its arsenal full and 27 ships under construction – but the events eventually led to wide-scale sacking, the *bucintoro* was reduced to a mere pontoon and the vessels sank while still tied to their moorings. A complex that was so extraordinarily important both in functional and symbolic terms could not *not* have its own artistic and architectural characteristics. Because of its commemorative and symbolic status, perhaps the most important example is the main doorway. This is the first example of Renaissance style in Venice, and it was completed in various stages. It was begun by Gambello in 1460 (when the Greek marble columns and the beautiful Veneto-Byzantine capitals were put in place), added to in 1571 (when it was raised and the winged lion commemorating the victorious Battle of Lepanto was added), and finished in 1687 after Morosini's victorious Peloponnesus campaign (the two large Greek lions were added, along with the terrace and gates with their eight allegorical statues, which replaced the bridge on the little *rio*). Another noteworthy example is the Sanmichieli building and "Le Gaggiandre", that is the two large roofs built over the Rio by Sansovino in 1543.

Special mention should also be made of the walls and towers surrounding the Arsenale, which Le Corbusier compared to the Kremlin in their ability to completely characterise the area for the visitor.

61. Church of San Pietro in Castello

The lagoon was first settled during the 5th and 6th centuries on the little island of Olivolo, strategically facing north and south along two strips of land. It would seem that there was already a fortified castle on the island to defend the island-city against attacks from the sea, and that a church dedicated to Saints Serge and Bacchus was added in the 7th century. The Bishopric of Venice was established on the island in 775.

After centuries of antagonistic relations, the Patriarch of Grado moved to Venice, where he shared jurisdictional powers over Venice with the Bishop of Castello (the regulations governing this novel example of "job sharing" were set out by the Republic itself). A Papal Bull brought the two posts together under the aegis of the Patriarchal Seat of Venice in 1491. The city's first Patriarch was Lorenzo Giustiniani.

For the entire Republican period, the centre of religious authority remained on the island, within the Sestiere of Castello, which had taken its name from the old fortress. There are conflicting explanations for the etymology of the word *Olivolo*, however: some maintain that there was originally an olive grove on the island; others that the name derives from the shape of the island; and others still that it ultimately comes from the Greek *pagos oligos* ("small castle"), via *olivolensis* and hence *olivolo*.

The church of Sergio e Bacco, which was no longer considered appropriate for a cathedral, was replaced in the 9th century and rebuilt in 1120 after it had been destroyed by fire. The architectural characteristics of the complex, as can be clearly seen in Jacopo de' Barbari's project, which consisted in a three-nave building, with a tripartite façade and semicircular apses, annexed cloister, bishop's residence and baptistery. In the 16th century, the Patriarch Antonio Diedo, decided to renovate the entire complex, and called for Palladio. Work on the building, which strangely enough began with the façade, were carried out by Palladio until he died in 1580, after which it was completed by his followers Smeraldi and Grapiglia in

1621. The façade, faithful to Palladio's original plans, is completely covered in Istrian stone, as is the *campanile*.

The *campanile*, a slightly hidden and solitary figure, is by Mauro Codussi. It is different from the original design because the original topping cupola was replaced in 1670 by an octagonal drum. The Patriarch's residence and its 16th century cloister link the body of the church to the *campanile*.

If you arrive via Calle Larga di Castello, the complex looks to all extents like a fortress, with its wooden bridge recalling the old castle's protective function. It is interesting to note that in the year 1000, after the Huns had attempted to attack Venice from the Lido, it was decided to construct a large defensive wall that went all the way from Olivolo to Santa Maria Zobenigo (or Santa Maria del Giglio), and an enormous iron chain was attached to the two towers in the vicinity of the Abbazia di San Gregorio to stop enemy vessels from gaining access to the Grand Canal. The entire complex was dismantled in 1379.

In the grass-covered *campo*, the paved walkways form functional links between the various access points. Other Venetian *campi* had similar walkways, but now there are only strips of marble that trace slightly absurd, but nonetheless fascinating, geometries.

In 1807, San Pietro di Castello was demoted from Patriarchal Seat and the residence was turned into a barracks. Its ancient splendour is revived during the traditional feast of the patron saint, when the "Corso", or traditional parade of boats and vessels, gives vent to the inhabitants' pride in their navigational skills. For the rest of the year the area is isolated (it is one of the furthest-flung areas of the city). At the very end of Via Garibaldi (quite rightly called "Via", or Street, as it has lost much of its old Venetian flavour), there is still an ancient Venice, an as-yet incomplete urban scheme similar to those found in older prints – a slightly older, slightly anachronistic Venice.